DUELING IN THE OLD SOUTH

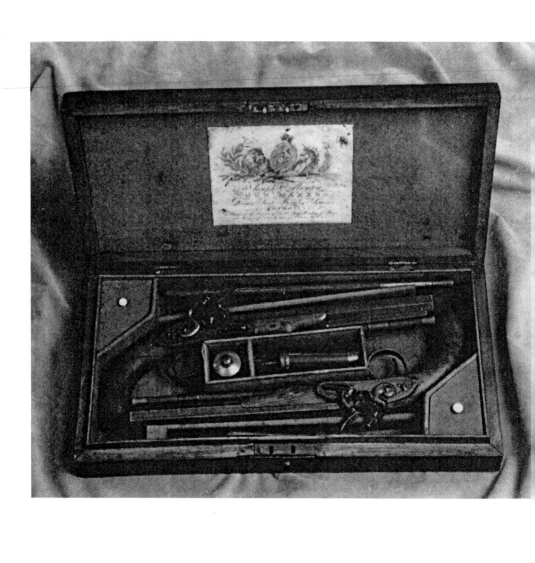

DUELING IN THE OLD SOUTH

Vignettes of Social History

By
Jack K. Williams

TEXAS A&M UNIVERSITY PRESS
College Station and London

Library of Congress Cataloging in Publication Data

Williams, Jack Kenny, 1920–
    Dueling in the Old South.

    Bibliography: p.
    1. Dueling—Southern States—History. 2. Southern States—
Social life and customs—1775–1865. I. Title.
F213.W72   394.8   79–7414
ISBN 0-89096-098-4 (cloth)
ISBN 0-89096-193-x (pbk.)

Manufactured in the United States of America
FIRST PAPERBACK EDITION

To my grandson Oliver Teel,
a citizen of the New South

Contents

Preface

AMERICAN Southerners, between 1800 and 1860, could well have resided in Charles Dickens' two cities—for they, the Southerners, lived in the best of times, the worst of times, in an age of wisdom, an age of foolishness, a season of light, a season of darkness. One who reads or writes about these Southerners is caught in this quandary of good-bad and finds himself alternately pro-con, love-hate, defend-condemn.

This little volume on dueling is an example, speaking of necessity, I believe, with a forked tongue, mixing frontier crudeness and aristocratic nicety, disrespect for law and independence of spirit, defense of honor and perversion of honor, sadism and amiability, courage and cowardice, and so on. The ambivalence adds spice to Southern history as a rule and, I hope, does not detract from the dueling story.

In my book I define the Old South to exclude Arkansas and Texas, and little research was done on Kentucky or Tennessee. The first two states are frontier so far as dueling is concerned, while the latter two are more "Old Southwest" than Old South. South Carolina and Georgia were the states where dueling had its largest following, aside from Louisiana's sword fighters.

DUELING IN THE OLD SOUTH

1

The Duel:
An Old-South Institution

FIRST on the scene, shortly after sunup, was the challenger, riding in a high-wheeled carriage with his "friend," or second, and a physician. Another surgeon came alone, in a light gig. Moments later the challenged arrived in a wagon, driven by his second. A bed had been laid in the wagon, which was to serve as an ambulance should one be required.

Everyone was in formal dress. One man wore "ballroom clothing—lace ruffles at his coat lapels, silk stockings, patent pumps." Another was clothed in "black pantaloons, a white vest and a cloth swallowtailed coat." The physicians were businesslike, having their sleeves rolled up and carrying forceps and tourniquets.[1]

The duelists said their good mornings with curt civility, then looked away. Their seconds busied themselves. They selected the dueling ground, choosing level land near the riverbank, clearing it of small brush. Walking together, they stepped off ten paces with slightly exaggerated strides. Pegs were driven at the spots where the shooters would stand.

Each second loaded his man's two pistols. Each duelist would carry to the line a single pistol. The extra was for a second round of shots, should such be called for.

A coin was tossed for position and word (the right to call out firing commands).

---

[1] The account of this incident is taken from Henry W. Lewis, "The Dugger-Dromgoole Duel," *North Carolina Historical Review* 34 (1934) : 336–338.

The doctors stood near the ambulance wagon. The duelists moved to their pegs, pistols by their sides, pointed toward the earth. The seconds located themselves equidistant between the fighters, out of the line of fire, each fully armed.

The second who had won the "word" explained his procedure. He would ask if the principals were ready, he said. Silence would indicate readiness. Then he would call out, *"Fire—one—two—three—stop!"* He would hesitate about a second between each word, he warned, and "should either of you fire before the word 'fire' or after the word 'stop' he falls by my hand."

Everything being understood, the word was given. Each duelist raised his arm, cocked, aimed, fired quickly. The sounds of the shots commingled, and no one present could say afterwards who fired first.

There was a rustle of startled birds, then thick silence. The smoke lifted. A combatant sank slowly to his knees and fell heavily, face down. The doctors rushed to him. One remembered later that even in so brief a time his face had lost its color, his lips had started to turn blue.

"Is he badly hurt?" someone asked. "I fear he is, Sir," one of the doctors answered. "I do not think he will live. . . ."

This was the 1837 duel between Congressman George Dromgoole and hotel owner Daniel Dugger, fought near Gaston, North Carolina. With sundry variations, this unhappy scene was repeated time and again throughout the antebellum South. It was a scene played out often enough to be commonplace in Dixie prior to 1825 and less than rare, certainly, between then and the end of the Civil War. It was the *Code Duello*, the "affair of honor," the Southern gentleman's method of settling personal disputes and avenging insults to self, family, or friends.

Writers about the American South have always found in the formal duel a kind of fascination and have drawn from it their own moralism—if they believed it at all. Some, like Arthur Scott, dismissed dueling as an infrequent, unimportant aberration; but such observers were few. Arthur Hudson wrote about the tragic humor and pathos in the duel, calling it "as grim as Steele in earnest or Swift in jest, as matter-of-fact as Fielding . . . as romantic as Dumas. . . ." Louis Wright defined the duel as "heroics dear to popular romance . . . a refinement of chivalry. . . ." Robert Remini, one of Andrew Jackson's many good biographers, saw the duel as a mechanism designed to display macho—to prove honor, fearlessness, implacability in the face of insult.[2]

Clement Eaton, greatest of the Old South's historians, believed the duel to be evidence of the military-mindedness of Southerners and of their cult of virility. Eaton and numerous other writers viewed the duel as clear evidence of the disinclination of Southerners to use the courts in connection with personal matters. They cited the advice Andrew Jackson's mother had given her famous son, "Never tell a lie, nor take what is not your own, nor sue anybody for slander or assault and battery. *Always settle them cases yourself!*"[3]

John Hope Franklin, premier chronicler of American slavery and author of the excellent book *The Militant South*, has worked the whole matter of the duel neatly into his thesis that nineteenth-century upper-class Southerners were violent men, made so by the "peculiar institu-

[2] Arthur P. Scott, *Criminal Law in Colonial Virginia* (Chicago: University of Chicago Press, 1930), p. 178; Arthur P. Hudson, *Humor of the Old Deep South* (New York: Macmillan Co., 1936), p. 409; Louis B. Wright, *The Cultural Life of the American Colonies* (New York: Harper & Row, 1957), p. 6; Robert V. Remini, *Andrew Jackson* (New York: Harper & Row, 1966), p. 42.

[3] Clement Eaton, *A History of the Old South*, 3rd ed. (New York: Macmillan Co., 1975), pp. 3, 110, 396–397; W. H. Sparks, *Memories of Fifty Years*, 3rd ed. (Macon, Ga.: J. W. Burke & Co., 1870), p. 148.

tion" of slavery. This violence was practiced in accord
with class levels, he said—typified by the whipping of
Negroes, the caning of yeomen, and formal dueling with
assumed equals. Franklin also spoke neatly and well for
those who viewed the duel as something of a puberty rite
for planters' sons or as a catalyst to quick success in politics, law, or love.[4]

Be all that as it may, the duel is an exciting chapter
in the social history of the pre Civil War Southerner.
More than exciting, it is a chapter adding credibility to
theories about the Southerner's rigid class structure,
exaggerated sense of honor, lingering classic romanticism,
and reluctance to be confined by the letter of the law.
Even if not illustrative of such qualities, the dueling story
is nonetheless worth telling simply for the rich history
in it.

Formal dueling in America flourished only in settled
civilization, not on the frontiers. That is to say, dueling
did not arrive with the first home seekers but awaited the
consolidation of settlement. Additionally, formal dueling
caught on mainly through emulation. Visiting Frenchmen
along with German and English army and navy officers
enjoyed the duel and taught its concepts to Americans.
Thus, American dueling assumed significant proportions
only after the Revolutionary War period.[5]

The duel in America was never epidemic except in
the South, and there only in the coastal plains—those
areas of cotton culture and plantation eminence where
slaveholding was common, romanticized aristocracy was

[4] John Hope Franklin, *The Militant South* (Cambridge: Harvard University Press, 1956), pp. 33-61.

[5] Clement Eaton, *The Freedom of Thought Struggle in the
Old South* (New York: Harper & Row, 1964), p. 52; Franklin,
Militant South, p. 44.

in flower, and much of the nation's early history was determined.

This is not to say that formal dueling was unknown outside the South. Duels between gentlemen were recorded in New York, Illinois, Pennsylvania, Massachusetts, and elsewhere in the North, New England, and the Northwest. But the duel was never really established in those areas, and antidueling legislation there won quick acceptance.

The duel traveled with low-country Southerners into the hill country and beyond, but frontiersmen and mountain people were disinclined to accept the trappings of written codes of procedure for their personal affrays. They improvised and substituted. In place of the formal duel at ten paces, with its exchanges of notes, employment of seconds, and restrictions on weapons, they adopted knife fighting (sometimes while tied to each other, arm to arm), quick-draw shootouts, eye gouging, nose biting, and informal, generalized bushwhacking.[6]

Thus the formal duel, fought usually in close obedience to an accepted body of rules, based on European practice but tempered by local custom, was for the most part a facet of life only in the Old South. In the coastal deltas of these eastern states and along the river valleys, formal dueling reached its fullest strength and maintained its ugly vigor long after it had all but disappeared elsewhere. The reasons for this are no doubt numerous,

---

[6] For illustrations, see Don Seitz, *Famous American Duels* (Freeport, N.Y.: Books for Libraries Press, 1966; originally published by Thomas Y. Crowell, 1929), p. 29; J. Cooper, *Notions of the Americans*, 2 vols. (London: Colburn & Co., 1828), 2:394–396; Jack K. Williams, *Vogues in Villainy* (Columbia: University of South Carolina Press, 1959), chap. 2; Carl Bridenbaugh, *Myths and Realities: Societies of the Colonial South* (New York: Atheneum, 1976), chap. 3; Bertram Wyatt-Brown, ed., *The American People in the Antebellum South* (West Haven, Conn.: Pendulum Press, 1973), chap. 5.

but all are undocumented. That the duel represents a note-worthy epoch in the social history of the explosive South is indisputable. Why it developed is subject to sociological-psychological guesswork, an intellectually risky business.

Statistics on dueling in the South are imperfect at best, but enough sources exist to indicate that "honorable altercations" were frequent. Sixty-three duels were described by a writer dealing with the Savannah area between 1800 and 1840, and the editor of the Camden, South Carolina, *Gazette* attached no particular importance to his matter-of-fact announcement in 1817 that three fatal duels had occurred in his town during the week.[7]

One observer declared that New Orleans in the early 1800's registered "three or four duels a day" and that at least one of the best citizens of the venerable city "came to old age with a proud record of participation in fifty duels." While this is probably exaggerated, New Orleans was the queen city for dueling and did have some famed resident duelists, one of whom could document by recall each of twenty-four duels in which he had been a principal.[8]

In Mississippi in the 1840's, duels were said to be "as plenty as blackberries," with Vicksburg and Clinton considered headquarters cities for the activity.[9]

Southern newspapers are excellent and ready sources

[7] William L. King, *The Newspaper Press of Charleston, S.C.* (Charleston: Edward Perry, 1872), pp. 164–166; Camden (S.C.) *Gazette*, September 22, 1817.

[8] Harnett T. Kane, "River People, River Ways," in *This Is the South*, ed. Robert Howard (New York: Rand McNally & Co., 1959), p. 202; John S. Kendall, "According to the Code," *Louisiana Historical Quarterly* 23 (1940): 145–146; Fairfax Downey, *Our Lusty Forefathers* (New York: Charles Scribner's Sons, 1947), p. 258; Harriet Martineau, *Society in America*, 3 vols. (London: Saunders & Otley, 1837), 3:55–56.

[9] Franklin, *Militant South*, pp. 11, 38–39, 42; Hudson, *Humor in the Old South*, pp. 429–430.

for information on the number of duels, although they are not complete records, since duels did not all make newspaper copy.[10] Papers for the 1800–1860 period leave no doubt that the duel was a regular and violent occurrence. If the editor was favorable to dueling or to the victorious duelist, he might headline his story "Unfortunate Affair," "Unhappy Transaction," or "Lamentable Affray." Should he be antiduel or a friend of the victim of the duel, his heads would read "Horrid Murder," "Cowardly Assault," or "Dastardly Assassination."[11] Sometimes the account was printed with names, sometimes without.

Dueling was not often carried to the county or district courts for trial; hence court records and court rolls are generally silent about its prevalence. Grand juries, on the other hand, sometimes gave space to dueling in their quarterly presentments. Grand jury statements may have had little effect on the incidence of dueling, but they do suggest its frequency and its seriousness. An example is the presentment of a Savannah, Georgia, jury in 1819. Jury foreman Steele White wrote, "The frequent violations of the law to prevent duelling have made the practice fashionable and almost meritorious among its chivalrous advocates. . . . Viewing the subject, as we do, of such magnitude, we deem it our duty to present [the matter]. . . ."[12]

Travelers to the South from abroad wrote much of duels they witnessed or heard about. Their travel diaries and volumes are rich sources of information not only on dueling but on sundry aspects of Southern social life. Such credible foreign visitors as William Faux, James

[10] Thomas Gamble, *Savannah Duels and Duellists, 1733–1877* (Savannah: Review Publishing and Printing Co., 1923), pp. 135, 154. A manuscript in the Yates Snowden Papers at the South Caroliniana Library, University of South Carolina, lists fourteen "ungazetted" Charleston duels.

[11] Hudson, *Humor in the Old South*, p. 410.

[12] Gamble, *Savannah Duels*, p. 135.

Silk Buckingham, Fanny Kemble, and Frederika Bremer were amazed at public tolerance of the duel. Faux, for instance, said he had been introduced to thirteen different duelists, eleven of whom "had killed a man each." They were, he said, "proud birds of a feather." Buckingham wrote that Southern citizens "shrugged off" duels as "manifestations of manly spirit." One duel had taken place while he visited in Columbia, South Carolina, he said. Two young men had exchanged shots at twelve paces, each wounding the other. "The parties then withdrew from the combat," he wrote, "but no notice was taken of the affair by the public authorities, and with the community it excited no sensation beyond the passing hour."[13]

Traveler James Cooper was perplexed not so much by the number of duels in cities like Charleston as by the number in small towns. Charles Janson thought the duels resulted from the Southerner's "strict notions of *honor, and a good name.*" John Melish and a German baron name Axel Leonhard Klinkowström advised their readers that the duel was so frequent in the South and so much a part of Southern life that, in the baron's words, "a visitor should be careful of what he says and what society he keeps." Baron Klinkowström repeated a story that illustrated the traveler's potential danger. "Some young English travellers had gathered," he wrote, "openly and art-

---

[13] William Faux, *Memorable Days in America* (London: Simkin & Marshall, 1823), pp. 47, 89–90; James S. Buckingham, *The Slave States of America*, 2 vols. (London: Fisher, Son & Co., 1842), 1:552; 2:3–4. See also Frances A. Kemble, *Journal of a Residence on a Georgia Plantation in 1838 and 1839* (New York: Harper & Bros., 1863), pp. 249–250; Charles Lyell, *A Second Visit to the United States of North America*, 2 vols. (New York: Harper & Bros., 1849), 2:31–32; James Stirling, *Letters from the Slave States* (London: John W. Parker & Son, 1857), pp. 266–273; Tyrone Power, *Impressions of America*, 2 vols. (London: Richard Bentley, 1836), 2:130.

lessly to scorn America and its authorities. . . . A certain Colonel D—— got wind of such conversation . . . and took the opportunity to reproach these men seriously and sharply for their improper conduct and their ill-considered expressions. As Colonel D—— was known to be able to clip off a light at a distance of twenty feet, with the bullet from a pistol, these men had the sense to keep quiet. . . ." Klinkowström concluded that "the many and decisive duels testify to an unruliness in the American character."[14]

Harriet Martineau, famous authoress and world traveler, agreed with that evaluation. The "hubbub" of dueling, she wrote, was prevalent and symptomatic of both the "false idea of honour" and "the recklessness of life . . . not confined to the semi-barbarous parts of the country. . . ." She cited data given her about New Orleans duels. "It is understood," she wrote, "that in New Orleans there were fought, in 1834, more duels than there are days in the year, fifteen on one Sunday morning; that in 1835, there were 102 duels fought in that city between the 1st of January and the end of April; and that no notice is taken of shooting in a quarrel. . . ." She concluded, "The spirit of caste, and the fear of imputation, rage. . . ."[15]

One telling indicator of the amount of dueling in the South is a listing of well-known men who admitted to having been involved in such contests. Dozens of congressmen, several state governors, numerous newspaper editors and publishers, and a host of prominent planters were duelists. Among them were George Poindexter, Mississippi

---

[14] Cooper, *Notions of the Americans*, 2:394–396; Charles W. Janson, *The Stranger in America, 1793–1806* (New York: Burt Franklin, 1971; originally published in 1807), p. 368; F. D. Scott, ed., *Baron Klinkowström's America, 1818–1820* (Evanston, Ill.: Northwestern University Press, 1952), pp. 45, 79.

[15] Martineau, *Society in America*, 2:60; 3:55–56.

governor and territorial delegate; renowned senator Henry Clay; the remarkable John Randolph of Roanoke; United States president Andrew Jackson; Confederate States vice-president Alexander Stephens; William L. Yancey, fire-eating Alabama congressman and cheerleader for states' rights; Benjamin F. Perry, celebrated South Carolina trial lawyer and newspaper editor; Sam Houston of Tennessee, Kentucky, and Texas fame; senator Thomas Hart Benton; Button Gwinett, constitutional father from Georgia; John Sevier, Tennessee statesman; William Crawford, eminent Georgian; and Armistead Mason, Virginia state legislator and aristocrat.[16] The list could be lengthened (and will be below), but the point is clear. The duel did indeed amount to a social institution, at least among the upper classes, in the Old South.

[16] Seitz, *Famous Duels*, pp. 18–22, 118–119, 124–129, 170; Harnett T. Kane, *Gentlemen, Swords and Pistols* (New York, William Morrow & Co., 1951), chaps. 3–15; Richard McLemore, *A History of Mississippi*, 2 vols. (Hattiesburg, Miss.: University College Press, 1973), 1:238ff., 296–297; Eaton, *Freedom of Thought*, 53; Marquis James, *The Raven: A Biography of Sam Houston* (Indianapolis: Bobbs-Merrill Co., 1929); Wayne Gard, "The Law," in *This Is the South*, p. 103.

2

Grounds for a Challenge

FORMAL duels in the South had their origin in a multitude of specific causes. These ranged from political differences and unhappy business relationships to presumed insults about family, friends, or physical, mental, or moral traits. As one observer noted, "The smallest breach of courtesy, no matter how unintentional; the slightest suggestion of unfairness in a business deal; even a moment's awkwardness—were sufficient grounds for a challenge." Or, as an especially verbose traveler to Virginia wrote:

> An offence which elsewhere would be regarded as one of homeopathic proportions, is very apt to assume in Richmond the gravity of colossal dimensions; even a coolness between parties is dangerous, as having a fatal tendency speedily to ripen into a deadly feud. Once arrived at this point, a personal encounter is inevitable, unless, to avoid it, one party or the other is induced to quit the city. It is curious enough to witness the cool and matter-of-fact way in which even the ladies will speculate upon the necessities for, and the probability of, a hostile meeting between such and such parties, and in which, when they hear of a duel, they will tell you that they long foresaw it, and that it could not be avoided.[1]

The dueling rate for Richmond—low, comparatively speaking—indicates that if a mere "coolness between parties" caused duels there, other Southern cities were no less vexed with the problem of trivial beginnings for potentially tragic confrontations. Indeed, the situation generally must have been like that supposedly reported

[1] Kendall, "According to the Code," p. 145; Alex[ander] Mackay, *The Western World; or, Travels in the United States in 1846–47*, 3 vols., 3rd ed. (London: Richard Bentley, 1851), 2:75–76.

by a member of Louis XVIII's bodyguard, who said he had fought three duels in a single day. One opponent had looked askew at him. Another had looked him full in the face, but with a hard glance. The third has passed him by without looking at him at all.

As would be expected in so volatile a period as 1800 to 1850 and in so sensitive an area as the antebellum South, arguments over politics were frequent. Southerners took politics seriously. In some ways party affiliation was akin to church affiliation, and membership in a party, like that in a church, might result in schisms or the formation of splinter groups. Each such group naturally claimed sole legitimate relationship to the mother organization, and discussions on this point brought forth more heat than light.

In Savannah, for instance, an observer declared that "in this little community there are no less than six classes of politicians. We have the Republicans, Aristocrats, Aristocratic-Republicans, Republican-Aristocrats, Democrats, and a few called Hell-Fire Republicans, and when three or four of the different classes meet, by chance . . . they never leave off disputation as long as there is a drop in the bottle. . . ."[2]

This combination of hot politics and strong drink led to duels, formal or otherwise. As early as 1803, for example, two duels in Savannah were described by a Savannahian to a Maryland friend with this conclusion: "Politics was the cause of both of these duels—the Republicans are not to be trifled with in this part of the world."[3]

George Dromgoole and Dan Dugger, whipped to a frenzy by party followers, fought their North Carolina duel in 1837 over Whig-Democrat differences. Whig-

---

[2] Gamble, *Savannah Duels*, p. 83.
[3] Ibid., p. 117.

Democrat conflicts of philosophy also led to the death of Congressman Jonathan Cilley at the dueling pistol of William Graves, Kentucky colonel and newspaperman.[4]

The question of whether Texas should be annexed as a state brought a challenge from T. L. Clingman of North Carolina to William L. Yancey, Alabama congressman and hothead.[5]

Abolition and lack of consensus over the right or wrong of slavery caused duels from the 1830's forward. Sergeant Prentiss, a Yankee turned Southerner with a vengeance, fought a number of Mississippi duels over slavery. Because of his liberal editorials, John Pleasants, antislave editor of the *Richmond Enquirer*, was goaded into a duel and killed. The Pleasants duel illustrates the intensity of hatred engendered by the abolition issue. Pleasants and his younger opponent agreed to special rules for their fight. Each man would carry two pistols and a knife. One pistol would be fired on command, then each man would advance toward the other, firing the remaining pistol at will and using the knife if necessary.[6]

The nullification controversy was another matter that raised tempers past the boiling point. An argument over the correctness of John Calhoun on this issue brought a Georgia gentleman death at the hand of one of Calhoun's admirers. In other nullification duels, Mississippi governor George Poindexter shot an opponent, and South Carolina lawyer Benjamin Perry killed Turner Bynum, a newspaper editor. Perry and Bynum fought in 1832 on a small river island, and it is a commentary on the public acceptance of dueling that thereafter Perry could con-

[4] Lewis, "Dugger-Dromgoole Duel," pp. 331–332; Seitz, *Famous Duels*, pp. 251–282.

[5] Seitz, *Famous Duels*, pp. 310–314.

[6] Eaton, *Freedom of Thought*, p. 263; *De Bow's Review* 29 (1860): 505–507.

tinue to hold positions of honor and trust in state government.[7]

For that matter, a number of public figures gained prominence and were pushed ahead in their careers because of prowess in dueling. Georgia's governor William Crawford moved into the public limelight because of his well-publicized duel with land speculator Peter Van Alan in 1804. The remarkable Sam Houston was much applauded because of his success in a Kentucky duel with General William White. To his credit, nonetheless, Houston told his followers that he was not in favor of the duel as a method of settling disputes and hoped dueling would be successfully outlawed. Despite this admission, his reputation as a ready fighter remained with him and did him no political harm.[8]

In Mississippi, one writer noted, it was understood as late as 1850 that one rarely reached the pinnacle of political success unless he had displayed his macho—his masculinity—in a duel or some other accepted mode of personal warfare.[9] Whatever the truth to that, it is unlikely that any Southerner, in Mississippi or elsewhere, engaged in a duel solely to enhance his political career. On the other hand, the widespread social acceptability of the duelist was a factor which no doubt predisposed a political figure not to back away from a challenge.

The number of state legislators, congressmen, governors, and other public officials who had dueling records lends credence to a view of the importance of a fighter's

[7] Sparks, *Memories*, pp. 85–91; McLemore, *Mississippi*, 1:238–243; Benjamin Perry Diary, Southern Historical Collection, University of North Carolina at Chapel Hill; Lillian A. Kibler, *Benjamin F. Perry, South Carolina Unionist* (Durham, N.C.: Duke University Press, 1946).

[8] Stephen Miller, *Bench and Bar of Georgia*, 2 vols. (Philadelphia: J. B. Lippincott & Co., 1858), 1:218; James, *The Raven*, pp. 66–67; Scott, *Klinkowström's America*, p. 45.

[9] Franklin, *Militant South*, pp. 38, 50.

image to a man's career. Added to those earlier mentioned, a list of dueling legislators and state executives includes Mississippi governor Henry Foote, who fought at least three duels in his native state and one in Alabama, Virginia senator A. T. Mason and Virginia representative John McCartey, who killed each other on the dueling field in 1819, and Georgia governor James Jackson, who killed the state's lieutenant governer because the latter had accused him of having an overbearing disposition. North Carolina congressman Robert Vance was killed by fellow legislator S. P. Carson in 1827 (Carson was reelected three times thereafter), and George McDuffie, South Carolina congressman, was wounded in an 1827 duel. Virginia congressman William Lewis survived a duel when his pocket watch stopped a bullet he received from Colonel T. H. Cushing. Thomas Marshall, a Kentucky legislator, won fame dueling an anti-Southern Yankee in 1842. The death in a duel of popular North Carolinian R. D. Spaight resulted in the passage of an early Southern antidueling law. The reputation of South Carolina lawmaker James Blair as an expert shot was confirmed when he wounded a challenger in the presence of onlookers, who had laid bets on the outcome. Finally, there was Judge Daniel Huger of South Carolina, who as a young man just elected to the legislature took dueling pistols to the capital with him—and was promptly forced by the Columbia city fathers to post a sum of money to "bind him over to keep the peace."[10]

[10] Ibid., pp. 50–53; Seitz, *Famous Duels*, pp. 21, 109, 118, 281; John D. Wade, *Augustus Baldwin Longstreet* (Athens: University of Georgia Press, 1969; originally published in 1924), p. 21; Samuel Ashe, *History of North Carolina*, 2 vols. (Spartanburg, S.C.: Spartanburg Reprint Co., 1971; originally published by L. Van Noppen, 1908–1925); 1:92–94, 184–185, 306–307; J. Marion Sims, *The Story of My Life* (New York: D. Appleton & Co., 1884), pp. 92–94; Samuel G. Stoney, ed., "The Memoirs of Frederick Adolphus Porcher," *South Carolina Historical and Genealogical Magazine* 44

Of course, any list must include three political giants
mentioned earlier: Andrew Jackson, Henry Clay, and
John Randolph of Roanoke. The latter two dueled with
each other over foreign policy matters. They met on the
Virginia side of the Potomac on an April morning in
1826. Each fired once and missed. Second shots were called
for. Clay fired first, again missing his target. Randolph
then discharged his pistol in the air, and the two national
leaders left the field on a friendly note.[11]

Andrew Jackson, for his part, was dueling's highest
ranked participant, for the record does not charge any
other American president with having been an active
duelist. James Armstrong, one of Jackson's numerous
enemies, once listed fourteen duels or fights in which
Jackson had engaged. He concluded, however, that fourteen was an inadequate figure. "The list [now] in my possession has accumulated to nearly ONE HUNDRED FIGHTS
or *violent and abusive quarrels*," he said.[12]

Jackson's best-remembered duel was with Charles
Dickinson. While drinking with companions one evening,
Dickinson made uncomplimentary remarks about Rachel
Jackson, Andrew's wife, who was the subject of much
gossip. The following day Jackson confronted the twenty-
seven-year-old man and, despite an attempted apology,
demanded "a gentleman's satisfaction." The two met on
the dueling field in May, 1806. Eight paces were measured

(1945) : 79; Seitz, *Famous Duels*, pp. 310–314; Eaton, *Freedom of
Thought*, pp. 179–180, 263; Gamble, *Savannah Duels*, pp. 83, 117;
McLemore, *Mississippi*, 1:238–240, 296–297; Robert R. Howison,
"Duelling in Virginia," *William and Mary College Quarterly His-
torical Magazine*, 2d ser. 4 (1924) : 225–226; Wade, *Longstreet*, p.
21; Allan Nevins, *The Diary of John Quincey Adams* (New York:
Longmans, Green & Co., 1928), p. 24.

[11] Hugh Garland, *The Life of John Randolph of Roanoke*, 2
vols. (New York: Greenwood, 1969; originally published in 1854),
2:260.

[12] Cited in Franklin, *Militant South*, p. 272.

off. At the single word "Fire!" Dickinson aimed and shot. His ball hit Jackson in the chest but Old Hickory did not fall. Instead, he raised his left arm and pressed it against his wound, then raised his right arm slowly, aimed, and squeezed the trigger. The hammer stopped at half-cock. Jackson, bleeding badly, drew it back and fired again. Dickinson was killed. Jackson recovered, to become judge, general, and president—and to fight more duels.[13]

Jackson dueled with Dickinson because of a woman. Other duels were fought throughout the South for the same reason. Some observers wrote that Southern women took pride at being fought over and agitated duels through open flirtation. Others believed that men dueled because they thought that women would not be interested in a man who was afraid or unwilling to fight. A spokesman for the flirtation school wrote that one clear cause of the duel was "found in jealousies concerning women." Men, he said, were "lashed into frenzies . . . by the habits of flirtation practiced by only too many of the beautiful and fascinating belles of Virginia."[14]

The view that a woman might not care for a man unwilling to duel when challenged had implied support, at least, from the wife of a Clinton, Mississippi, man who told him on the eve of a duel that she would "rather be the widow of a brave man than the wife of a coward." And in another instance, a second had heard that the duel in which his friend was involved might be called off because the opponent had been taken ill. He visited the sick man's home to ask if he would be present for the fight. "If he is not there," declared his spirited wife, "I will take his place."[15]

---

[13] Remini, *Jackson*, pp. 42–43.

[14] Howison, "Duelling in Virginia," p. 221.

[15] Charles Brough, *Historic Camden*, Publications of the Mississippi Historical Society, 7 (Oxford, Miss., 1903): 290; Hudson, *Humor in the Old South*, p. 431.

One tragic encounter over women was that between William Gohlson and Albert Jackson of Memphis. A woman of some social significance had caused an understandable stir in town by lashing another woman with a horsewhip on a Memphis street. The lasher accused the lashee of having slept with the former's male slave. Barroom talk about the incident was ribald, apparently, and Jackson, the whipped woman's cousin, challenged Gohlson, one of the tellers of tales. At the duel each managed a single shot at the word "three," and each killed the other.[16]

Duels over women in New Orleans could have a different perspective or rationale. There, it was whispered, some gentlemen had quadroon mistresses, kept in cottages or rooms near Rampart Street. Occasionally these women in their ménages à deux were attracted to other men, and their "protectors" fought duels as a result.[17]

In Virginia two cousins loved the same girl and dueled over her, with injury only to their masculine prides. But another Virginia duel over a woman was more typical as to both origin and result. In this instance William Glasswell was attending a ball with a friend when a man named Ritchie, "disordered by wine," insulted the woman in some way. A duel followed, and Ritchie was killed.[18]

Duels over women were usually reported in the newspapers, but not in such complete details as those about politics, and the name of the woman was never mentioned or given away by other reference. An English traveler to the South thought that even mentioning such duels was unnecessary and indelicate. He retold the story of a nameless man who had "detected" another male making a "clan-

---

[16] Kane, *Gentlemen, Swords and Pistols*, pp. 115–120.
[17] Downey, *Lusty Forefathers*, pp. 260–261.
[18] Howison, "Duelling in Virginia," pp. 228–231.

destine visit" to his wife. A duel resulted, of course, and justice triumphed—the clandestine lover was wounded. "This unfortunate event should not have found its way into these pages," the traveler wrote, "had it not already passed the comment of American editors."[19]

Occasionally a story about a shooting match caused by unrequited love or some variation of a romantic relationship did receive full press coverage. Such was the case in Charleston, South Carolina, when a theater manager dueled a male ballet dancer—but here the situation was not one involving socially ranked gentlemen. The account of the duel noted that the combat was

> . . . between two "stage-struck heroes;" the subject—all subduing love! The theatrical duellists were Placide, the manager of the Charleston company . . . and one of his troup, named Douvillier, a ballet-dancer. The manager kept a lady of whom the performer was also enamoured; on which the "green-eyed monster" took possession of the breast of Placide, who, however, was uncertain as to the actual commission of the injury he suspected. At length . . . the commander had demonstration of his being *brutified*. A challenge was given. . . . A place was appointed, and the next day, *at noon*, fixed for the combat. Before the time arrived, half of Charleston were apprised of the circumstance; and the combatants went to the ground, attended by multitudes to witness the event.[20]

The insult, real or presumed, explicit or uncertain, about women or anything else, was the classic call to a Southern duel. As noted previously, to insinuate that a man used the truth loosely or to make disparaging remarks about a man's family, friends, business, church, political beliefs, status in society, or physical appearance was to invite a challenge.

[19] Janson, *Stranger in America*, p. 369.
[20] Ibid., pp. 369–370. See also Kane, *Gentlemen, Swords and Pistols*, pp. 121–125; Ashe, *North Carolina*, 2:224.

Of the insults recorded by history, some were printed in newspapers, some were given verbally, and some were posted on the walls of buildings. An example of a strong printed jibe is that directed to John Black by William Cline, via the Charleston, South Carolina, press. Wrote Cline: "I can only account for Mr. B's petulance, by ascribing it to the effects of age upon a naturally weak mind." A duel followed promptly, as was the obvious intent.[21]

Another insult meant to force a duel appeared in the Savannah *Republican* in 1809: "I hold Francis H. Welman a Liar, Coward and Poltroon. John Moorhead." A longer and more pungent insult was printed at about the same time in the Savannah *Gazette*, describing a local citizen as a man with a "contracted phiz and phlegmatic constitution; the features of his countenance appear clouded with malignant passion; his soul is prone to false invective; and though the insidious smile should now and then relax the furrows in his brow it bears no claim to benevolence."[22]

An unusual but effective verbal insult was offered to William Bay by Thomas Crofts during an argument. In a moment of high anger, Crofts called Bay an *"ugly, gawky, Yanke looking fellow. . . ."*[23]

Insults were often minor league. Charles Lucas fought a duel with Thomas Benton because Benton had called him a puppy. The stilted, formal challenge resulting from this episode of so little importance illustrates the tragicomedy of the dueling aristocracy. Lucas wrote: "Sir—I am informed you applied to me on the day of the election the epithet 'puppy.' If so, I shall expect that satis-

[21] Charleston *Courier*, July 2, 1824.
[22] Cited in Gamble, *Savannah Duels*, p. 132.
[23] Paul R. Weidner, ed., "The Journal of John Blake White," *South Carolina Historical and Genealogical Magazine* 43 (1942): 114.

faction which is due from one gentleman to another for such an indignity."[24]

Benton, incidentally, was an innovative, compulsive insulter. Fortunately for him, not all his barbs brought challenges. On one occasion, at a political rally, he told his opponent to turn to the audience. Then to the audience he said, "Citizens, this is not the profile of a man; it is the profile of a dog!" At another meeting he presented three members of the opposition with these words: "Why, here are———, ——— and———, as demure as three whores at a christening."[25]

An Alabama man, about to lose the object of his arduous courtship to a titled foreigner, chastised his enemy by calling him "Count No-Account, Baron—of intellect." This resulted in a duel, and the baron was shot in the face.[26]

In New Orleans, residents awoke one day to find this notice printed in their morning papers:

> If the contemptible puppy, Charles A. Luzenberg, who has long humbugged the community with false ideas of his courage, but who has always succeeded in shuffling off his responsibility upon third persons, is at all anxious to enjoy the privilege of a shot, he can obtain one by applying to: J. S. McFarlane, Corner Poydras and Circus Streets. N.B. No substitutes admitted.[27]

Anyone who traveled to the South or from one part of the South to another needed to be aware of local custom regarding the definition of an insult. A comment that might pass unnoticed at home could bring a quick challege elsewhere. Sir Henry Morton Stanley was explaining this to his readers when he wrote that in New Orleans one could "give and take, assert an opinion and hear it

---

[24] Cited in Seitz, *Famous Duels*, pp. 128–130.
[25] Kane, *Gentlemen, Swords and Pistols*, pp. 185–186.
[26] Ibid., pp. 10–13.
[27] Ibid., p. 35.

contradicted without resort to lethal weapons but, in Arkansas, to refute a statement was tantamount to giving the lie direct, and was followed by an instant appeal to the revolver or bowie." Stanley's view of the liberality of antebellum New Orleans was contradicted by others, though, one of whom said that in New Orleans the "rage for duelling is at such a pitch that a jest or smart repartee is sufficient cause for a challenge. . . ."[28]

The trick, apparently, was to know well with whom you were jesting and exchanging repartee and to understand clearly how sensitive the subject matter of the jest or repartee might be.

A man might be forgiven an insult if he claimed he had indulged too much in strong drink, but only if he made an admission of lack of recollection of the wrongdoing, accompanied by the statement, "I believe the party insulted to be a man of the strictest veracity and a gentleman." The most popular dueling code explained all this in these words: "Intoxication is not a full excuse for insult, but it will greatly palliate. If it was a full excuse, it might well be counterfeited, to wound feelings or destroy character." In general, then, "insults at a wine table . . . must be answered for."[29]

The basic cause of the duel was a slur on a man's character, the injuring of a man's reputation—matters that today would probably be handled by a legal suit. One should note, however, that antebellum state courts were for the most part powerless to defend against slander or damaging insinuation, because of a widely held belief that

[28] Dorothy Stanley, ed., *Autobiography of Sir Henry Morton Stanley* (Boston: Houghton Mifflin Co., 1909), p. 157; George Eggleston, *The Warrens of Virginia* (New York: G. W. Billingham Co., 1908), p. 31.

[29] John L. Wilson, *The Code of Honor; or Rules for the Government of Principals and Seconds in Duelling* (Charleston: James Phinney, 1838, reprinted in this volume), p. 16.

courts ought not be called on to solve personal problems. As a Tennessee lawyer wrote, "Questions affecting personal character were rarely referred to courts of law. . . . To carry a personal grievance into a court of law degraded the plaintiff in the estimation of his peers and put the whole case beneath the notice of society."[30] So long as this view was held by the gentleman class of the South, the duel remained an acceptable substitute for the judiciary—and a social problem of significant proportions.

[30] F. D. Srygley, *Seventy Years in Dixie: Recollections and Sayings of T. W. Caskey and Others* (Nashville: Gospel Advocate Publishing Co., 1893), p. 310.

3

A Matter of Class:
Who Dueled

As its proponents insisted, recourse to the formal duel may have helped put an order of civility into Southern life—at least at the higher social levels. A gentleman fought another gentleman with a pistol on the field of honor, according to the rules. A gentleman horsewhipped or caned a person of the lower estates.

The notion that gentlemen caned or horsewhipped men of lesser social status had symbolic significance. Any person hit with a cane or lashed with a whip was being told in a very rough and public way that he did not rank as high as his attacker; hence the importance of the choice of weapons by Southern senator Preston Brooks for his merciless attack on New England senator Charles Sumner in Washington in 1856.

Sumner, in a speech, had used such words as harlot, pirate, falsifier, assassin, and swindler to describe elderly South Carolina senator Andrew Pickens Butler. Preston Brooks, Butler's nephew, sought out Sumner and is reputed to have said: "Mr. Sumner, I have read your speech carefully, and with as much calmness as I could be expected to read such a speech. You have libeled my State, and slandered my relation, who is aged and absent, and I feel it to be my duty to punish you for it." The punishment followed, and Sumner was caned senseless. The people of Massachusetts, and of New England generally, were properly angered—but, as historian Charles Sydnor has written, it is doubtful they understood the delicate shades of meaning implicit in Brooks's actions.[1]

[1] Charles Sydnor, "The Southerner and the Laws," *Journal of Southern History* 6 (1940) : 22–23.

Dueling, then, was a matter of class, and the "field of honor" was often called the "field of equality." No gentleman ever accepted a challenge from one not considered his social equal.

But who was his social equal? The rules of society did not always make this clear. Laboring men and mechanics were not classified as gentry. Businessmen and merchants were suspect, except that bankers were usually highly considered. Military officers with the rank of captain or above were gentlemen, of course, as were preachers—except that circuit-riding Methodist and Baptist ministers were often considered outside the pale, especially during the early antebellum years.

Military rank, in particular, was a mark of distinction and much sought after. Most Southern men with social position had military titles. Travelers to the South were quick to note this ostentatious attribute of Southern gentility and commented on it in their writings, usually with some amusement. Visitor Henry Latrobe, the architect, wrote that every Southern male was a captain, colonel, or general. "We have here Colonel Tom and Colonel Dick and Major Billy," he wrote. Englishman James Silk Buckingham recalled that the main banker in Savannah was a colonel, as was the city's principal bookseller. The innkeeper was a major—"and Captains abound in every class." Bishop Whipple noted in his diary that every third Southern man "was blest with a military handle to his name."[2]

College teachers were counted as gentlemen, except sometimes in the eyes of recalcitrant students. At the University of Virginia, for example, in 1839, a professor

[2] Benjamin Latrobe, *The Journal of Benjamin Latrobe* (New York: D. Appleton, 1905), p. 24; Buckingham, *Slave States*, 2:192–193; Henry Whipple, *Bishop Whipple's Southern Diary, 1843-44*, ed. Lester Shippee (New York: D. A. Capo Press, 1968; originally published in 1937), p. 82.

was horsewhipped in the presence of perhaps a hundred bystanders. One college professor of mathematics at the University of Georgia accepted a challenge from a student's brother in 1853, but the duel was averted. The professor had accused the student of dishonesty.[3]

At the Virginia Military Institute in 1852 an angry senior challenged professor T. J. Jackson, saying the professor had insulted him during a lecture. Rather than engage in a duel, the professor brought court martial charges against the student, who was dismissed from school. Had the challenge been accepted, the Confederate States of America might not have had its famed general Stonewall Jackson.[4]

Students, as well as teachers, were sometimes accounted socially worthy of dueling among themselves. Two South Carolina college students dueled in 1833, following a trivial dining hall dispute. One, James Adams, was killed. His opponent was maimed for life. Two of the state's political leaders were seconds in this duel involving boys not yet out of their teens—"a curious example," one writer says, "of young and old mingling in a common cause."[5]

Planters were gentlemen—the very embodiment of the class—but mere ownership of land did not make one a planter. Some insisted that title was earned by the ownership of at least twenty slaves—twenty slaves, a planter,

[3] Joseph Kett, "Order and Disorder among Youth," in *The Private Side of American History*, ed. Gary Nash, 2 vols., 2nd ed. (New York: Harcourt Brace Jovanovich, 1975), 1:267; Sims, *Story of My Life*, pp. 88–91.

[4] Douglas S. Freeman, *Lee's Lieutenants, A Study in Command* (New York: Charles Scribner's Sons, 1942), 2:703–704.

[5] Daniel W. Hollis, *University of South Carolina: South Carolina College* (Columbia: University of South Carolina Press, 1951), pp. 92–93; W. E. Walker, "The South Carolina College Duel of 1833," *South Carolina Historical and Genealogical Magazine* 52 (1951): 140–142; Wade, *Longstreet*, p. 315; Kett, "Order and Disorder among Youth," 1:257.

fewer than twenty, a farmer. But that is an insufficient definition. A planter had both the tangible qualities of possession and the intangible ones of courtly manners and a precise understanding of what was a gentleman's province and what was not. He had reverence for the past. He cherished the concepts of pride and personal dignity, whatever his surroundings. He epitomized noblesse oblige, hospitality, public service, and honor—honor above all else.

So not all landowners were planters, just as not all were gentlemen. But all, or nearly all, aspired to be. They felt they could rise to the rank, as had John C. Calhoun before them. Hence they worked to acquire more land, more slaves, more of the exterior polish they believed they needed—and, should honor demand it, they dueled.[6]

The social status of newspaper editors was debatable. Some observers considered them gentlemen; others did not. As a result of this ambiguity, a number of Southern editors were caned or whipped rather than dueled, and others were caned, then dueled. Xenophon Gaines, crippled editor of the *Georgia Express*, was savagely beaten by Augustine Clayton. Editor J. Hueston of the Baton Rouge *Gazette* was caned first and later invited to a duel, as was Melzer Gardner of the Portsmouth, Virginia, *Chronicle*. Elias Bondinot, famed editor of the *Cherokee Phoenix*, was threatened not only with a caning, but with being kidnapped and sold for a slave.[7]

Benjamin F. Perry, a South Carolina legislator who had been an editor himself, passed judgment on his erst-

---

[6] See Sydnor, "The Southerner and the Laws"; Clement Eaton, *The Growth of Southern Civilization, 1790–1860* (New York: Harper Torchbooks, 1961), chaps. 6–12; Eaton, *A History of the Old South*, chaps. 4, 10, 21, 23.

[7] Louis T. Griffith and John E. Talmadge, *Georgia Journalism, 1763–1950* (Athens, Ga.: University of Georgia Press, 1951), pp. 33–35, 57; Frederic Hudson, *Journalism in America* (New York: Harper & Bros., 1873), pp. 762–768.

while colleagues with these words: "I am not going to challenge any blackguard of an editor. The next man I fight or challenge shall be a man of distinction. I am done with lackeys. There is no honor to be acquired in a contest with such men, and I am unwilling to become their executioner."[8]

However, the threat of a challenge to an editor for a stand he had taken in his paper was real enough that it dampened the ardor of much of the press. Although some editors pumped up their courage and wrote what they pleased, many chose instead elaborate politeness in their references to local citizens.

Examples are numerous. One editor wrote, "Our correspondent will excuse us for not publishing his notice as it contains an implied charge of a very serious character against an individual." Another editor, having printed a note from Henry Britton that he no longer intended to honor his wife's debts, felt constrained to add: "It is with regret that we communicate the above advertisement, but as impartial conductors of a paper, we are bound to give it a place. The well known character of Mrs. Britton will however, exonerate her from any illiberal insinuations which would arise from it under other circumstances."[9]

The publishers of the *Columbian Museum* in Savannah printed a general disclaimer. "We do not attempt to regulate or criticise the language of our advertising customers," they wrote; "we should hope, therefore, in future, to be spared the trouble of being considered in any respect as parties between persons who may chuse to apply to each other (through the medium of our paper) the most scurrilous or indecent epithets."[10]

The pleas and disclaimers did little good. Publishers

8 Kibler, *Perry*, p. 145.

9 Charleston *Courier*, April 14, 1838; Camden (S.C.) *Gazette*, February 13, 1817.

10 Cited in Gamble, *Savannah Duels*, p. 100.

and editors were held responsible for all that appeared in their pages, regardless of authorship. There is considerable truth in an antebellum cartoon that portrayed the editorialist with a pen in one hand and a dueling pistol in the other.[11]

Frederick Marryat, popular English traveler to America, declared that "the majority of the editors of the newspapers in America are constantly practising with the pistol, that they may be ready when called upon, and are most of them very good shots." "In fact," he added, "they could not well refuse to fight, being all of them colonels, majors, or generals—'tam Marte quam Mercurio.' "[12] Whatever the degree of exaggeration in Marryat's account, numerous Southern editors were duelists. Editors in Georgia, Tennessee, and Louisiana resorted to the duel. At least eleven Mississippi editors were principals in shootouts by the code, and three of them were killed. No fewer than six Virginia and six South Carolina editors fought duels. Two of the Virginians and two of the South Carolinians died of their wounds.[13]

Number one among the editor-duelists was O. J. Wise of the *Richmond Enquirer*. William and Mary–educated, onetime attaché with United States legations in Berlin and Paris, Wise fought at least eight formal duels. Un-

---

[11] Eaton, *Freedom of Thought*, p. 169. Also see Griffith and Talmadge, *Georgia Journalism*, p. 38.

[12] Frederick Marryat, *A Diary in America with Remarks on Its Institutions*, ed. Sydney Jackman (New York: Alfred A. Knopf, 1962), p. 161.

[13] Lester Cappon, *Virginia Newspapers, 1821–1935* (New York: D. Appleton Century Co., 1936), p. 14; Griffith and Talmadge, *Georgia Journalism*, pp. 34–38; Kibler, *Perry*, p. 145; McLemore, *Mississippi*, 1:296, 418; Jack K. Williams, "The Code of Honor in South Carolina," *South Carolina Historical and Genealogical Magazine* 41 (1953): 116; Eaton, *Growth of Southern Civilization*, p. 276; Howison, "Duelling in Virginia," pp. 240–242; Seitz, *Famous Duels*, pp. 29–30.

believably, he never hit an opponent, and he was never wounded.[14]

A runner-up to Wise in the number of duels fought, and outclassing him in the number of street fights, was Dr. James Hagan, editor of the Vicksburg, Mississippi, *Sentinel*. A doctor of medicine from Philadelphia, he moved south, turning from the healing sciences to divisive journalism. As editor of the *Sentinel* he had several so-called desperate encounters, including some duels—one with the editor of the *Whig*, Vicksburg's competing paper. He was himself gunned down in 1843 by the son of a judge about whom he had written unkind remarks. Hagan carried a pistol with him most of his adult life, although he was not armed when he was killed. His fights were many and varied. An account of one of his rencontres noted that he had ended the affair by "laying his antagonist to the land."[15]

Dr. Hagan's *Sentinel* was a newspaper with a tragic, violent history during the years from its inception in 1836 until the Civil War. During its first years its editors were involved in a series of duels and brawls over the paper's position on a widespread cotton-speculation controversy. In 1842 *Sentinel* writer James Fall was wounded in a duel with the president of the Railroad Bank occasioned by an uncomplimentary story. In 1846 *Sentinel* editor T. E. Robins was shot at ten paces by J. M. Downes, and a few days later Robins' replacement as editor, Walter Hickey, was challenged by Downes's second. Hickey killed the challenger in the duel that followed.

Thereafter the paper's editors and assistant editors fared badly, one after another. Editor James Ryan was killed by the publisher of the competing *Whig*; Walter Hickey was shot in his second duel as a newspaperman,

[14] Eaton, *Growth of Southern Civilization*, p. 276.
[15] Hudson, *Journalism in America*, pp. 762–763.

recovered, went to Texas, and was killed in a fight there; and editor John Lavins was jailed for writing threatening editorials. A man named Jenkins, who followed Lavins as editor, was murdered, and his successor, F. C. Jones, committed suicide.[16]

A Baton Rouge, Louisiana, editor was involved in one of the longest and meanest duels in the pre–Civil War period. In August, 1843, the editor, J. Hueston, wrote a piece scathingly derogatory to Louisiana congressman Alcée Labranche. The two men fought a duel after Labranche had hit Hueston with a cane. The New Orleans *Diamond* described the affray as if it were a championship prizefight:

> The distance agreed upon was forty yards, and the weapons selected were double-barreled shotguns, loaded with ball. The parties fired between the words one and five. They fought four rounds.
>
> *First round.* Mr. Labranche discharged both barrels at the same time, and before Mr. Hueston had fired a second barrel the time fixed upon expired. Of course he lost a fire.
>
> *Second round.* Both fired single barrels at intervals. Mr. Labranche's second ball struck the pantaloons of Mr. Hueston, and passed through the knees of them without touching the flesh.
>
> *Third round.* Mr. Labranche fired both barrels at the same time; the balls passed through the hat of Mr. Hueston about two inches apart.
>
> *Fourth round.* Mr. Hueston fired first. Mr. Labranche's shot took effect in the left side, on the last rib, and passed out on the other side; ranging low down. He threw his gun forward and fell back at full length on the ground. The wound was pronounced fatal by the physicians in attendance. He expired shortly after, in full possession of

[16] Ibid., pp. 763–764.

his mental faculties. The parties exhibited on the ground the utmost coolness and fortitude.[17]

Even writers on the paper might incur the wrath of unhappy readers and be challenged. As an example, in New Orleans in 1858, the drama critic of the *Daily Delta*, Emile Hirairt, offended several gentlemen admirers of a singer with his caustic comments concerning her performance. Faced with a number of challenges, he accepted two of them, and arrangements were made to duel these representatives of the group on succeeding days. Pistols were used the first day, and each duelist missed. Shotguns were chosen for the second day's event. Hirairt killed his challenger and was himself injured.[18]

Writers, editors, professors, and planters had no monopoly as duelists. All professions were represented at the duel. Now and then even preachers sent and accepted challenges. Two ministers of the gospel who were duelists or almost-duelists were from South Carolina and Georgia. The Carolinian, an Episcopalian rector, went through all preliminaries, including the acceptance of a challenge. But at that point he was forced to post a peace bond, and the affair ended. The Georgian, the Reverend J. H. Ingraham, was said to have been a duelist. At any rate, he carried a pistol with him in the pulpit under his robe and was killed by the accidental discharge of the weapon when he was adjusting his clerical garb before services.[19]

On rare occasions medical doctors were principals in duels. Generally these events were brought about by professional disputes between physicians. Doctors Samuel Chopin and John Foster, staff physicians at New Orleans'

---

[17] Ibid., pp. 764–765.

[18] Kendall, "According to the Code," pp. 154–155.

[19] Edward H. Folk, "The Code Duello in South Carolina" (M.A. thesis, University of South Carolina, 1924), pp. 37–38; Seitz, *Famous Duels*, p. 113.

Charity Hospital, met in a duel after an argument over which of them had prescribed proper treatment for a patient. Chopin was wounded but soon recovered.[20]

At the same hospital, colleagues charged Dr. Charles Luzenberg with malpractice. Infuriated, Luzenberg challenged in order three physicians, a newspaper editor, and a lawyer. The lawyer agreed to the challenge, but the duel did not take place. This was the source of Luzenberg's reputation as a coward, mentioned earlier.[21]

One much-told tall tale was of a nameless physician-duelist reputed to have been an unusually expert shot. He maintained his skill as a marksman, it was said, by hanging up cadavers at the hospital and firing at them.[22]

Formal dueling was a male aberration in the Old South, and stories of females engaged in personal warfare on the field of honor are no doubt as apocryphal as that of the doctor who hung cadavers. One anecdote that has found its way into Southern literature tells of two females who had challenged each other and had reached the dueling ground. Once there, however, "they dropped their weapons, and the encounter degenerated into hand-to-hand combat. They kicked, clawed and pulled out one another's hair. Finally the lustier virago managed to gain a grip on certain of her rival's anatomical features. . . . She was prevented from tearing them from her squealing adversary only by the timely arrival of the police."[23]

Another tale, which may have had truth in it, concerned the Southern woman who in 1850 was said to have issued a challenge to a Carrolton, Georgia, man, charging him with "grossly and villainously" slandering her name

---

[20] Kane, *Gentlemen, Swords and Pistols*, pp. 23–26.
[21] Ibid., pp. 30–36.
[22] Ibid., pp. 23–24.
[23] Downey, *Lusty Forefathers*, p. 265.

and with spying on her at night. He would not accept the challenge and demanded that she be arrested on a charge of intent to murder.[24]

Finally, there is the account of the Tennessee patriot who, in 1861, sent forth a general challenge directed to her sisters in the North. As printed in a Memphis newspaper, the challenge read:

A CHALLENGE

Where as the wicked policy of the president—Making war upon the South for refusing to submit to wrong too palpable for Southerners to do. And where as it has become necessary for the Young Men of our country, My Brother in the number to enlist to do the dirty work of Driving the Mercenary from our sunny South. . . .

For such indignity offord to Civilization I Merely Challenge any abolition or Black Republican lady of character if there can be such a one found. . . . To Meet me at Mason's and dixon line: with a pair of Colt's repeaters or any other weapon they may Choose. That I may receive satisfaction for the insult.

Victoria E. Goodwin
Springdale Miss April 27, 1861[25]

A few duelists were professionals—fighters famed for their shooting abilities, much like the quick-draw experts of the West. According to a contemporary, these skilled duelists were "usually detested by the better part of the community but . . . everywhere tolerated. . . . I have known a half-dozen in my time and they were all bad citizens, the dread and reproach of society."[26]

One such man arrived in Charleston, South Carolina,

[24] Hudson, *Humor in the Old South*, pp. 480–481.
[25] Ibid., p. 480.
[26] Samuel G. Stoney, ed., "The Autobiography of William John Grayson," *South Carolina Historical and Genealogical Magazine* 49 (1948) : 28.

in the mid-1950's. Rumor credited him with having killed two adversaries in duels and reported him as being quick to anger. Rumor became fact when he took a dislike to a young Charleston lawyer, goaded him into a duel, and killed him with one quick shot. Six friends of the deceased barrister then vowed to avenge the death of their companion by dueling the murderer, one at a time, until some member of the six should be successful. They drew lots for first honor, but the stranger killed this man too with apparent ease. The society of requiters thereupon disbanded. As one of the group later said: "We gave it up. We agreed that nobody stood a ghost of a chance before him. . . . So we decided to let the monster go, and trust to the Almighty to cut short his career . . . [but] he lived to be an old man and died peacefully in his bed."[27]

This particular duelist, it was said, came to the dueling grounds with a smile on his face. Prior to taking his position, he would carefully place a cigar on a nearby stump or rock, saying he would be back to claim it before it burned out. So long as this man remained in Charleston, he was "neither ignored nor cut" and attended all major social gatherings.

Alexander Keith McClung of Kentucky was perhaps the South's best-known and most feared duelist. A nephew of John Marshall, cousin to the Breckinridge family, son of a prominent Virginia and Kentucky legislator and jurist, he should have been a Southern gentleman in the richest sense of the term. Rather, he was known as the "Black Knight of the South." He had an uncontrollable temper, drank heavily, and engaged in an endless series of fights. He had two duels in Uruguay, was wounded once in his left hand, fought one Mississippi duel at eight paces and

[27] Snowden Papers, South Caroliniana Library, University of South Carolina.

killed his opponent, and was responsible for the shooting deaths of at least seven other men. He challenged for minor slights and presumed offenses, it was said, and people shunned his company. He became a recluse because of his reputation, and when poverty overtook him he killed himself with one of his dueling pistols.[28]

McClung was feared and avoided. Others somewhat like him were set upon and driven away. "Big Luke" Manning, for instance, a dueler and brawler in Lexington, South Carolina, received a lynch-law sentence of banishment from his community. He had made the mistake of provoking a duel with popular Colonel Drury Sawyer, who was crippled. The terms of battle were that each man would take position with an empty rifle and, on signal, load and fire. In his haste, Colonel Sawyer got his ball stuck. "Big Luke" loaded skillfully, but before he could fire spectators overpowered him, beat him severely, and drove him from the county.[29]

A well-known duelist with quite a different reputation from that of Luke Manning was Jose Lulla, a wealthy Spanish resident of New Orleans. Lulla was famed with both sword and pistol. With the latter he was said to be able to shoot coins from between a man's fingers or an egg off a man's head. He was often challenged, always attempted to apologize, and if the apology was not accepted, fought the duel. Some men died at his hand; others were wounded. He himself died a natural death in 1888 at the age of seventy-three.[30]

[28] Kane, *Gentlemen, Swords and Pistols*, pp. 99–112; William O. Stevens, *Pistols at Ten Paces: The Story of the Code of Honor in America* (Boston: Houghton Mifflin Co., 1940), p. 111; Reuben Davis, *Recollections of Mississippi and Mississippians* (Boston: Houghton Mifflin Co., 1889), pp. 215–218.

[29] Edwin J. Scott, *Random Recollections of a Long Life, 1806 to 1876* (Columbia: Charles A. Calvo, Jr., Printer, 1884), pp. 127–128.

[30] Downey, *Lusty Forefathers*, pp. 263–264.

The ready fighter, the bully, and the professional duelist, respected or detested, were of little significance to the viability of the duel. Dueling depended strongly on those who gave faithful and sometimes mindless adherence to the trappings of social elitism, who paid open homage to controlled violence as being synonymous with both maleness and personal honor. The Southern gentry who fitted these classic ideals into the realities of their lives made up the bulk of those who fought the duel according to the book.

4

Honor among Duelers: Dueling's Rules and Procedures

JOHN LYDE WILSON, governor of South Carolina from 1822 to 1824, was author of a standard text, *The Code of Honor; or, Rules for the Government of Principals and Seconds in Duelling* (reprinted in this volume). His pamphlet, first printed in 1838 and reissued in 1858, was much used throughout the South. He compiled the rules for dueling, he wrote, because the duel would "be persisted in as long as a manly independence and a lofty personal pride, in all that dignifies and ennobles the human character, shall continue to exist." That being so, he added, his listing of proper rules would save lives—for the rules were drawn to prevent indiscriminate shooting and to require efforts at reconciliation.[1]

Governor Wilson's code was the longest and best organized of several pamphlets and booklets containing rules for dueling. In addition to devoting careful attention to details of the duel itself, Wilson advised his readers how they might avoid a duel without loss of face, when and how to issue appropriate challenges, and how to judge a reply to a note as being honorable or otherwise. The pamphlet contained extensive rules for the conduct of seconds—a section which Wilson believed made his work especially useful. Wilson himself was an experienced second and claimed that he had "restored to the bosom of many, their sons, by my timely interference, who are ignorant of the misery I have averted from them."[2]

[1] Wilson, *Code of Honor*, pp. 3–4.
[2] Ibid., p. 6.

In the appendix to his code, Wilson reprinted the sometimes-used Irish Code of Honor, adopted in 1777 at the Clonmel Assizes. Other compilations known by Southerners included the French Code, a detailed document consisting of eighty-four specific rules of conduct on the field, and the English Code, printed in 1824. Both the Irish and English codes discouraged the use of the sword as a dueling weapon on the ground that too few gentlemen were expert in its use.[3]

Southerners were also familiar with John McDonald Taylor's *Twenty-six Commandments of the Duelling Code*. This brief but adequate set of rules was much in vogue in the New Orleans area. Lesser-used booklets were Joseph Hamilton's *The Only Approved Guide through All the Stages of a Quarrel* and Henry Ware's *The Law of Honor*.[4]

Printed codes were not always sufficient, however; teachers of the dueling technique were also in demand. Although the sons of Southern gentlemen were taught to shoot by their fathers, special training in the use of the smoothbore pistol on the dueling ground was essential. This was true not only for the young men but for older ones as well. A refresher course and supervised practice were imperative for a nonprofessional who had just accepted a challenge. For, as visitor Frederick Marryat noted, dueling in America was no nick-on-the-cheek affair, no harmless symbolic exercise. As he wrote, "the worst feature in the American system of duelling is that they do not go out, as we do in this country [England], to satisfy honour, but with the determination to kill. . . . Imme-

[3] See Seitz, *Famous Duels*, pp. 40–47, for the French and English codes. The Irish Code appears as an appendix to Wilson's code, which is included in this volume.

[4] Heloise Cruzat, "When Knighthood Was in Flower," *Louisiana Historical Quarterly* 1 (1918): 367–371.

diately after a challenge has been given and received, each party practises as much as he can. . . ."[5]

New Orleans was the educational mecca for would-be duelists, but schools of sorts existed in most Southern cities. Additionally, some duelists learned their skills overseas. Virginian William Glossell, for example, was taught to shoot dueling pistols while a student in Scotland. After his return to Virginia, he killed a less expert adversary.[6]

Just as there were professional duelers, discussed previously, so there were professionals noted not so much for their own dueling prowess as for their ability to train others in the skill. Such men as South Carolinians John Ashe and John Wilson were experts on procedure. Ashe fought at least one duel, in which he wounded his enemy, but he is better remembered as an ever-ready second or adviser. In his later years he claimed to have acted in official capacity at "fifty-one difficulties between gentlemen."[7]

Another widely known trainer and adviser of duelists in the southeastern states was Chapman Levy of Camden, South Carolina. Levy had fought as a principal in several duels and had been wounded once. He made Camden his headquarters for duel training. Near the town there stood a life-size cast-iron statue, which was used in target practice by those planning a fight. Camden citizens grew accustomed to the sound of bullets ricocheting from the work of art, and they said that one who sent or accepted a challenge was "going to the iron man."[8]

[5] Marryat, *Diary in America*, pp. 161–162. See also Lewis, "Dugger Dromgoole Duel," pp. 333–335; Howison, "Duelling in Virginia," p. 226.

[6] Howison, "Duelling in Virginia," p. 229.

[7] Folk, "Code Duello," p. 4.

[8] Sims, *Story of My Life*, p. 97; T. J. Kirkland and R. M. Kennedy, *Historic Camden: Part Two, Nineteenth Century* (Columbia: The State Company, 1926), pp. 233–235; J. B. Angell, *The Reminiscences of James Burrill Angell* (New York: Longmans, Green & Co., 1912), p. 54.

Advertisements for dueling schools and courses of instruction regularly appeared in Columbia, South Carolina, newspapers. One notice in 1840 described a curriculum "in the various branches of self defense . . . calculated to give satisfaction."[9]

In New Orleans, during the 1830's and 1840's especially, a number of dueling academies flourished, many of them on Exchange Alley. Emile Cazére operated a fencing school, as did Gilbert Rosiére, but fencing was pretty much out of style in America, even in Louisiana, by the midpoint of the antebellum period. One New Orleans school for the duel was operated by a free black, Bosile Crokere. Regarded by some as the best *maitre d'armes* in town, he ran a popular establishment.[10]

One Major Dunn announced in the New Orleans *Picayune* in February, 1845, the opening of his school for fighters. He promised the student full instruction in firearms, "perfect knowledge of the cane" as a weapon, and the proper use of the sword in "cut and thrust" encounters. If a visitor to the city did not have time for the full three-week course, Major Dunn said, he would offer a more compact version, consisting of "Two Lessons Daily —Morning and Evening."[11]

Considering the high incidence of dueling in the pre–Civil War South and the complicated formalities involved, the Major Dunns, Bosile Crokeres, Chapman Levys, and John Wilsons were no doubt in demand. Wilson's rules made it abundantly clear that proper dueling was a gentleman's business, as hedged in by conventions and proprieties as any facet of stilted social activity.

[9] Columbia *Southern Chronicle*, October 9, 1840, cited by Susan M. Ficking, "Ante-Bellum Columbia," in *Columbia: Capital City of South Carolina, 1786–1936*, ed. Helen K. Hennig (Columbia: R. L. Bryan & Co., 1936), pp. 13–14.

[10] Franklin, *Militant South*, pp. 45, 271.

[11] New Orleans *Daily Picayune*, February 7, 1845.

The initial step in a formal duel was a polite note written by the person believing himself insulted, asking if the presumed insult had been intentional and inviting a written apology. A typical prechallenge note was that written to William Yancey by Thomas Clingman in 1845:

> Sir: In the course of your remarks today you declared that you wished to have nothing to say with one possessed of the head and heart of the gentleman from North Carolina, alluding, as I understand, to me, personally. I desire to know of you whether, by the use of that expression, you intended toward me any disrespect, or to be understood that I was deficient in integrity, honor, or any other quality requisite to the character of a gentleman.[12]

The answer to such a preliminary note either precluded or dictated further steps. The original note had to be answered, said John Wilson, unless it came from a minor, a criminal, a lunatic, a man in his dotage, or one who had previously proved himself a coward—that is, had earlier "been publicly disgraced without resenting it." Of course, no answer was required to a communication from anyone who was not a gentleman, and, should a note come from a stranger, one had "a right to a reasonable time to ascertain his standing in society. . . ."[13]

When an answer was forthcoming, if it was properly apologetic or if it stated unequivocally that no insult had been intended, some form of public notice was taken of it so that all interested parties might know that the matter had been disposed of, in what manner, and with what language. The public notice could be a newspaper item or a poster displayed at appropriate places. Sometimes the notices were prepared by seconds, sometimes by the principals themselves. In the case of Georgians R. R. Dancy and George Owens, the notice declared that Dancy had

[12] Seitz, *Famous Duels*, p. 310.
[13] Wilson, *Code of Honor*, p. 10.

not been insulted as he had originally thought and that therefore no duel was required. "Nevertheless," the note continued, "his [Dancy's] honor as a gentleman has been fully vindicated" and Owens' actions have "commanded . . . full approbation."[14]

Another form of notice was that prepared by would-be duelers McQueen McIntosh and John Hopkins. Their two-part "card" read:

> I withdraw my challenge to Colonel Hopkins, together with any and every expression which I may have used calculated to injure the feelings either of Mr. Hopkins or General Hopkins [his father], and without hostility I do implicitly believe them to be gentlemen, soldiers and men of honor. McQueen McIntosh.

> In consequence of the above signed McQueen McIntosh, I declare that my attack upon him was predicated upon a supposed insult at that time, viz., in Darien on the 31st August. John Livingston Hopkins.[15]

Unfortunately, the peace between the two men was short-lived. At their next encounter they forsook the niceties of the code and engaged in a street brawl with pistols and knives. McIntosh was killed and Hopkins' arm was shattered.

Notices placed in newspapers were generally less wordy and complicated than posters like the one prepared by McIntosh and Hopkins. An example is the advertisement placed in the Savannah papers by seconds for J. R. Sneed and S. P. Hamilton:

> Screven's Ferry, So. Ca.
> November 11, 1856

> In an affair of honor pending between Mr. R. Sneed and Mr. S. P. Hamilton, we, the undersigned, selected friends,

[14] Gamble, *Savannah Duels*, p. 286.
[15] Ibid., p. 144.

express our gratification that we have been enabled to make an adjustment of the difficulty between the gentlemen, which is honorable and satisfactory to both parties.

John Richardson
John M. B. Lovell[16]

A prechallenge note was never mailed. It was always delivered personally by a second. The reply was likewise entrusted to a go-between.

The delivery of a challenge by the second followed an unacceptable reply to the original note. The challenge, like the prechallenge document, was drafted in polite terminology. Not elaborate, it offered a terse statement of the case against the person to whom it was directed and asked for "a gentleman's satisfaction." An illustration is that sent by John Clark to William Crawford in 1806:

Sir—The various injuries I have received from you make it necessary for me to call on you for the satisfaction usually offered in similar cases. My friend, Mr. Forsyth, is authorized to make the necessary arrangements on my part. With due respects, I am, Sir

Your humble servant
John Clark[17]

Some challenges were less polite but still within the framework of the code, which stated that no man would be required to accept an "abusive" communication. Andrew Jackson once challenged a young lawyer, who had suggested that Jackson stretched the truth, with these words: "My character you have injured; and further you have insulted me in the presence of a court and a large audience. I therefore call upon you to give me [satisfaction] . . . and I hope you can do without dinner until the

---

[16] Ibid., pp. 239–240.
[17] Seitz, *Famous Duels*, p. 172.

business is done; for it is consistent upon the character of a gentleman to make speedy reparation. . . ."[18]

Occasionally a challenge also dictated terms of battle, thus usurping one of the second's duties. Such was the case when a challenger noted, "Colonel Lawless will receive your terms and I expect the distance [between us at the duel] not to exceed nine feet."[19]

It is not possible to estimate the percentage of challenges sent but not accepted. Certainly many were turned down, and a variety of reasons were given for nonacceptance. George Prentice of Louisville, Kentucky, refused a challenge with a note saying: "I have not the least desire to kill you, nor to harm a hair of your head, and I am not conscious of having done anything to entitle you to kill me. I do not want your blood on my hands, and I do not want my own on anybodys. . . ."[20]

James Jackson of Georgia, on the other hand, stated that he refused because of family obligations. He wrote, "The wife and five children—the sixth I have reason to believe will shortly be in existence—are powerful reasons to prevent engagements which may not only be fatal to myself, but those who have right to look to me for support."[21]

This resort to claims of family responsibilities was also used by the remarkable John Sevier of Tennessee when he refused a challenge by Andrew Jackson. Sevier had incurred Jackson's wrath when he said, reputedly, "I know of no great services [Jackson has] rendered his country except taking a trip to Natchez with another man's wife."[22]

---

[18] Cited in Kane, *Gentlemen, Swords and Pistols*, p. 120.

[19] Seitz, *Famous Duels*, p. 172.

[20] Kane, *Gentlemen, Swords and Pistols*, p. xiv.

[21] Gamble, *Savannah Duels*, p. 47.

[22] Seitz, *Famous Duels*, p. 124.

William Swain, a North Carolina newspaper editor, printed a challenge he had received and refused to accept, adding a paragraph or so of ridicule. A Tennessee editor followed suit, noting: "With such an affair I refuse to have any connection. I recognize no heathenish so-called code of honor."[23]

What usually happened in case of a refusal to duel was that the refuser was "posted." This meant that placards were tacked up about town or that space was purchased in local and area newspapers or both. In any event, the news that a fight had been turned down was broadcast, and repercussions were certain. One planter, after being posted, left town and "went to Texas." Another man, having been posted, returned to his plantation and was not seen in society for ten years.[24]

A typical posting read: "I proclaim to the world, that John Miller, refusing to accept my said message, has evinced himself a lyar, a scoundrel, and a cowardly assassin. Richard Heyleake." Another noted: "I do declare Seth John Cuthbert to be a coward. My reasons shall be made known in the Publick Gazette."[25]

Sometimes the man posted replied with a notice of his own. As an example, Henry Putnam ran this notice in a local paper: "Mr. J. Wood, having published me yesterday as a coward &C. the public will please to suspend their opinions till Thursday next when by a state of facts they will find him a liar, coward and no gentleman. HENRY PUTNAM." William R. McIntosh's reply to his poster was: "To the charge of cowardice, I have to reply . . . that I

[23] Eaton, *Freedom of Thought*, pp. 164–166; Seitz, *Famous Duels*, pp. 29–30.

[24] Faux, *Memorable Days in America*, pp. 47–48; Julian A. Selby, *Memorabilia and Anecdotal Reminiscences of Columbia, South Carolina, and Incidents Connected Therewith* (Columbia: R. L. Bryan & Co., 1905), p. 94.

[25] Gamble, *Savannah Duels*, pp. 55, 96.

never expect to establish a fair reputation by duelling with men who are unworthy the notice of gentlemen. I am always prepared to repel the assaults of an assassin. You have threatened violence to my person. At your peril make your vaunting true. WM. R. McINTOSH."[26]

These replies were generally ineffective, and most men chose to fight. Well-known Henry Laurens admitted that he considered dueling to be ridiculous; yet he fought at least two duels, always firing in the air. "More than once," he said, "I had bravery enough to stand and be shot at, but was too great a coward to kill any man." Henry Clay said essentially the same thing.[27]

Posting a man sometimes did what the challenge had failed to do. This was true, for instance, in the case of Preston Brooks and Louis Wigfall. Wigfall had posted Brooks's father. Brooks then challenged his father's accuser, and in the ensuing duel both men were wounded.[28] In another case, a posting resulted in four men's firing away at each other. As a witness recalled, "Whaley shot Boyce through and through; Boyce missed completely; Gregg shot Pinckney through and through; Pinckney's ball struck Gregg's knife in his vest pocket."[29]

Partially because of the fear of disgrace from posting, many challenges were accepted, not rejected; and once acceptance had been received, the seconds drew up terms of combat, making all decisions and arrangements. The principals to the duel simply gave approval to what was done. A letter to his principal from Hiram Haines, second for George Dromgoole, is illustrative:

[26] Ibid., pp. 96–97, 142.
[27] Cited in D. D. Wallace, *The Life of Henry Laurens* (New York: Putnam, 1915), p. 216. See also Eaton, *Growth of Southern Civilization*, p. 277.
[28] Folk, "Code Duello," pp. 22–23.
[29] Letter from D. W. Johnson to Edward C. Johnson, January 13, 1835, in *Proceedings of the South Carolina Historical Association*, 1939, pp. 26–27.

My Dear Friend: I have this day received a note from Mr.
T. Goode Tucker relative to the arrangements for the final
meeting between his friend Mr. Daniel Dugger and my
friend Geo. C. Dromgoole, some time called "General."
Mr. Tucker proposes that the meeting shall take place near
Gaston, No. Ca. *Agreed to.* He proposes that the usual
weapons (pistols of course) shall be used. *Agreed to.* He
proposes further, that Mr. D. wanting some further time
to settle his worldly affairs desires until the 1st of November to arrange them. *Agreed to. . . .*[30]

Once the Wilson code gained acceptance, the perva-
sive notion that the challenged reserved the right to select
weapons and dictate general conditions no longer held in
proper dueling. According to the code, to seek or accept
any advantage in a duel "was an offense against good
breeding which would disgrace any man."[31]

As the agents for the principals, seconds were responsible for agreeing to special or unusual conditions
regarding dueling procedures or the weapons to be used.
Most duels were fought at a distance of about thirty yards
(ten to twenty paces), with flint-fired, smoothbore, single-
ball pistols, between men who faced each other. The most
common deviation was the substitution of shotguns for
pistols. Generally when shotguns were used, both duelers
would be killed or wounded.[32]

For some duels special contracts were drawn, consisting of numbered rules and stipulations. Such a con-
tract was drawn for the contest between William Crawford and John Clark in 1806, and one was made for the
Thomas Clingman–William Yancey affair in 1845. The
Crawford-Clark rules called for the duel to be fought at

---

[30] Lewis, "Dugger-Dromgoole Duel," p. 333.

[31] Kendall, "According to the Code," pp. 141–144; Thomas Mc-
Caleb, *The Louisiana Book* (New Orleans: R. F. Straughan, 1894),
p. 76.

[32] For examples, see Gamble, *Savannah Duels*, p. 242; Kendall,
"According to the Code," p. 155; Franklin, *Militant South*, p. 56.

ten yards, the word to be "make ready—fire," a "snap or flash" to be considered a shot, and, to "prevent the possibilities of suspicion of wearing improper clothing, each party [was to] submit to an examination by the seconds of his opponent." Rules for the Clingman-Yancey duel stated that each principal would "be permitted to have on the ground a surgeon and three friends, all of whom must be unarmed."[33]

Although unusual, the rule about unarmed men had merit. A few years earlier a Vicksburg duel had turned into a wild mob fracas when spectators with weapons joined the fight. According to an observer, "Twenty gentlemen were ranged on a side to see fair play, but at the second fire the whole forty went into the melee with dirks and pistols, and a battle of the most desperate character was fought, during which three men were killed, and seven or eight combatants, including the surgeon of Col. B., wounded."[34]

Besides shotguns, other weapons—knives ("Arkansas toothpicks"), daggers, swords—were called for now and then, but only rarely. As noted earlier, the sword was a much-used dueling weapon in the New Orleans area during the eighteenth and early years of the nineteenth centuries, but it lost favor as Englishmen filled the territories and states. Many wealthy Creoles sent their sons to Paris for schooling, and these young men returned expert in swordplay. Among themselves they dueled with their rapiers, and the death rate from their encounters was low.[35]

---

[33] Seitz, *Famous Duels*, pp. 17–71, 119–120, 314–315.

[34] "Arrows from a Tourist's Quiver," *Southern Field and Fireside* 1 (1861) : [305].

[35] On the use of swords, see Martineau, *Society in America*, 3:56; Kendall, "According to the Code," pp. 155–156; Downey, *Lusty Forefathers*, p. 258; Hudson, *Humor in the Old South*, pp. 413–414.

Perhaps the most unusual call for a weapon was that presented to Bernard de Marigny (the gentleman said to have introduced the dice game "craps" to the United States). De Marigny challenged a blacksmith, contrary to the code, which specified that dueling was to be between men of equal social rank. The smith accepted, but with a demand that he be allowed to choose weapons—again a departure from the code. Permission was granted, and the blacksmith chose sledgehammers. De Marigny had his second call off the affair, saying it had all been only a joke.[36]

An imaginative departure from the rules was allowed in a Georgia duel between two aristocratic planters, John Bernard and William Patterson. Bernard was known to be an excellent marksman, whereas Patterson was not. In an effort to even the odds, the seconds agreed that the two men would stand twenty paces apart, with their backs toward each other. At the proper signal, they would wheel and fire. When the signal was given, Patterson, the poor shot, managed to kill his opponent.[37]

Georgia was also the scene of an unusual "moving duel," when Daniel Mitchell (later governor) and William Hunter (then mayor of Savannah) met in the early 1800's. Their seconds had arranged a disaster in which the duelists would fire first shots at ten paces, second shots at six, and so on. Hunter was killed on the second shot. When elected governor in 1809, Mitchell took up the cause of those opposed to dueling and signed a law, albeit an ineffective one, against the practice.[38]

On occasion the nature of a departure from standard procedures indicated the depth of hatred that had possessed the duelers. Englishwoman Fanny Kemble, in her unhappy book about life on a Georgia plantation, told the bizarre story of two Darien, Georgia, planters who, fol-

[36] Downey, *Lusty Forefathers*, pp. 262–263.
[37] Gamble, *Savannah Duels*, p. 216.
[38] Ibid., pp. 111–112.

lowing an argument over the ownership of a parcel of land, arranged a duel with the stipulation that the winner was to have the privilege of cutting off the loser's head and placing it on a pole in the center of the disputed acres. Miss Kemble did not continue her story to say whether the gruesome event took place.[39]

Standard procedure was for the seconds to select an appropriate place for the duel, decide what witnesses would be allowed, and agree to the rules of combat that would be followed. The selection of the dueling place was not difficult because most Southern cities had special locations informally set aside for dueling. In New Orleans, the favorite dueling ground, at the foot of Esplanade Street, was known as "The Oaks" or "Allard's Oaks." Consequently, from about 1834 until after the Civil War, dueling in New Orleans was called "meeting under the oaks." Prior to 1834 many New Orleans duels were held at Fortin Plantation, on property now said to be part of a race track. As the city grew and as dueling became less acceptable, the duelists fought at various spots along the shores of Lake Pontchartrain or outside the city along the banks of the Mississippi River.[40]

Vicksburg duelists also fought at spots near the river. In Memphis, a grove of trees on Hernando Road, a few miles south of the city, served the dueling fraternity. Virginians dueled at "Alum Springs Rock," two miles from Fredericksburg. The site of an old mill, it was described by an observer as "being shut in from ordinary view by small areas of surrounding forests, interlaced in many places by wild vines."[41]

In Savannah, many duels were fought on a small river island north of the city or at the "Old Jewish Burial

[39] Kemble, *Journal of a Residence*, pp. 249–250.

[40] Seitz, *Famous Duels*, pp. 114–120.

[41] Kane, *Gentlemen, Swords and Pistols*, p. x; Howison, "Duelling in Virginia," pp. 217–219, 229, 234.

Ground" outside the nineteenth-century city's boundaries. Some South Carolina duelers shot at each other on Savannah or Tugallo River islands. In Georgia and Alabama prior to 1830, numerous duels were fought in Indian Territory at the land of the Creek Nation, near "the High Shoals on the Appalachee." Tom Burnside and George Crawford, with their dueling parties, traveled four days to reach the haven of Indian country for their shooting contest.[42]

When the duelists and their associates arrived at the field, positions were staked, and a coin was flipped for position and the giving of firing signals. It was understood that one second gained the right to call out signals while the other won the privilege of choosing position. The seconds then loaded the pistols, each inviting the other to superintend the process—an invitation usually refused. Each second then placed a loaded pistol in his principal's "awkward hand" (the one not normally used for firing), and the adversaries took their places. Then, as one pessimistic dueler wrote, "the fatal moment had arrived which was to send one or both . . . unannointed and unannealed into the presence of an avenging God."[43]

A second called out "Ready!" The pistols were changed to the proper hand, and the shooting followed. No principal was allowed to leave his post until told to do so by his second, and no principal was to speak at any time to any person other than his second.

As a rule, those who came to watch duels were quiet, reports said. Occasionally, though, a spectator would give way to the excitement of the moment. An enthusiastic witness of the Ritchie-Pleasants duel called out from a

---

[42] Gamble, *Savannah Duels*, p. 116; Kendall, "According to the Code," pp. 141–144.

[43] Gamble, *Savannah Duels*, p. 144.

safe position behind a tree, "Shoot him, shoot him again."[44]

Spectators at one of Henry Foote's duels were so numerous that some climbed nearby trees in order to have a better view. "Get down," someone called out, "General Foote shoots wild you know."[45]

More than four hundred people came to watch the Isaac Caldwell–Sam Gwin duel near Clinton, Mississippi, in 1836, fought because Gwin had "hissed" at Caldwell. Large crowds of noisy, betting spectators from nearby towns attended one of Alexander McClung's duels at Vicksburg in 1836, where they watched McClung kill his opponent.[46]

John Wilson believed that nine of ten duels could have been prevented by diplomatic seconds, and perhaps he was correct. Certainly the selection of an able second was important. It was agreed, for instance, that the duel between Thomas Hudson and Arthur Smith could have been prevented without dishonor to either man, but their friends pushed the affair to a conclusion, and both men were killed. This was also true concerning the duel between Thomas Baker and Daniel Brown. Baker called Brown a "d——d saddlebag lawyer," and seconds chosen by the men refused to authorize peaceful settlement. The duel was not fought in accord with usual procedures. Baker and Brown took position back to back, walked five paces, turned, and fired. Both men were killed.[47]

John Pope, a visitor in South Carolina, told of his success in preventing a duel. He wrote, "I . . . happily terminated the Dispute to their mutual satisfaction, by decreeing, that they both possessed indubitable Courage. . . .

[44] Gard, "The Law," p. 103.
[45] Kane, *Gentlemen, Swords and Pistols*, pp. 44, 207.
[46] McLemore, *Mississippi*, p. 296.
[47] Stoney, "Memoirs of Porcher," pp. 28–29.

That Capt. Sweetman had been too *precipitate* and Capt. Robertson too *hasty*: —that they therefore . . . stand 10 Yards asunder, then advance to the Centre, make their Concessions at the same Instant, *protruding their dextral Hands, until they came into Contaction* . . . that they should then repair to the Hotel and take a *Compotation of a late Importation from the Madeira Plantation, in Corroboration of the* aforesaid *Pacification.*"[48]

Seconds for Edward Stanley, North Carolina congressman, and Henry Wise, Virginia lawmaker, were not as innovative as Pope, but they were equally successful in preventing an 1842 fight between their prominent friends. And a Georgia "affair of honor" in 1801 was reconciled by the seconds at the field just before the shooting was to begin.[49]

In the case of a Virginian whose seconds stopped his prospective duel, the report read: "About half past two o'clock yesterday afternoon the friends of the Virginian apologized for their friend—and from the popping of pistols the sound was changed to the popping of corks."[50]

A second might stop a fight—but also he might be forced to fight himself. For instance, if a second delivered a challenge which was refused on the grounds that the challenger was not a social equal, it was then the second's duty to offer himself in his friend's stead. Likewise, the second had to accompany his principal to the field and there see to it that all went fairly. One Southern duel was postponed because a second complained that the opposition's pistol was too long; another second forced a delay in a duel when he charged his friend's challenger with hav-

---

[48] John Pope, *A Tour through the Southern and Western Territories of the United States of North America* (Richmond: Arno Press, 1971; originally published in 1792), p. 86.

[49] Franklin, *Militant South*, p. 53; Gamble, *Savannah Duels*, p. 107.

[50] Cited in Gamble, *Savannah Duels*, p. 275.

ing a hair trigger on his weapon. In the case of a duel between one McQueen and a Captain McIntosh, a second refused to allow the principals to talk with each other at the field of honor. When the men began to exchange words, the second called out, "Gentlemen, *forbear to altercate!*"[51]

In the famous duel between Sergeant Prentiss and General Foote, the general's second objected to Prentiss' cane—used because the man had been lame for many years. The second's objection was based on a notion that, as Prentiss leaned on the cane and stood sideways, the cane was between him and his opponent and might "turn a ball." Prentiss tossed his cane away, stood on one foot, and managed to wound his opponent.[52]

Should there be a gross violation of rules—for instance, should a principal fire before the count or after it had ended—the second was expected to shoot him down. For that purpose each second was usually armed while at the scene of combat. Following a duel, should a second believe that a meaningful regulation had been disregarded by the opposition side, it was his duty to bring this to public attention, a task almost certain to provoke still another duel.[53]

According to the Wilson rules, any wound, however slight, meant that the duel was at an end and that "full satisfaction" had been taken, unless the wounded principal demanded another round. If this happened, the firing might well continue until a death resulted. The Irish Code

[51] Kane, *Gentlemen, Swords and Pistols,* pp. 176–177. The observer of the last event was actually referring to a duel between McQueen McIntosh and John Hopkins; he was confused about the names.

[52] "Arrows from a Tourist's Quiver," p. [305].

[53] See the exchange of letters between T. M. Stuart and A. M. Manigault concerning an 1853 duel between Manigault and J. D. Legare. The latter's second believed that not all the appropriate regulations had been followed (Snowden Papers, South Caroliniana Library, University of South Carolina).

did not allow this flexibility, saying that "any wound sufficient to agitate the nerves and necessarily make the hand shake, must end the business for that day."[54]

A duel could be declared ended with honor without a wound's being inflicted. Wether or not that happy state of affairs prevailed depended on the astuteness of seconds as well as the temper of the duelists. Most duelers apparently ended the contests after a single shot; others insisted on second and third attempts. Thomas Ap Jones of Mississippi, for instance, took three shots at and from his opponent, then insisted on more.[55]

A number of duelists pointedly chose to miss their targets. Such men might send or accept challenges, but once at the field they could not shoot directly at a man. Two Virginia duels illustrate the point. O. J. Wise and P. H. Aylett of Richmond met, all preliminaries having been accomplished. Then, as the story was told: "The word 'fire, one, two, three,' was given. Aylett standing with his pistol pointed at Wise and Wise with his pointing upward and neither fired—some explanation was asked. . . . The word was again given and Aylett fired at Wise (missing him) and Wise fired in the air."[56]

Arthur Morison and Richard Randolph had a similar battle. Morison had challenged Randolph, a lawyer, for commenting rudely on a decision made by a judge who was Morison's wife's uncle. At the duel which followed, Morison fired and missed. Randolph held fire until the last

---

[54] Wilson, *Code of Honor*, pp. 13, 20.

[55] Gamble, *Savannah Duels*, pp. 211, 243–246; Yorkville (S.C.) *Compiler*, September 12, 1840; Kane, *Gentlemen, Swords and Pistols*, p. 202; Charles Sydnor, *A Gentleman of the Old Natchez Region* (Durham: Duke University Press, 1938), p. 46.

[56] Diary quoted in Eaton, *Growth of Southern Civilization*, p. 276. The Irish Code specifically forbade this "dumb firing" or shooting into the air (see Wilson, *Code of Honor*, p. 19).

count, then fired in the air. The two men said they were satisfied and left the field.[57]

The Henry Clay–John Randolph duel followed a similar script. Clay shot first, his bullet going through Randolph's coat. Randolph fired into the air. Then, in violation of the no-talking rule, Randolph said, "You owe me a coat, Mr. Clay." "I am glad the debt is no more," Clay replied.[58]

Randolph's "you owe me a coat, Mr. Clay," may be contrasted with the angry words concluding a brawl between Melzer Gardner, editor of the Portsmouth, Virginia, *Chronicle*, and Mordecai Cook, a Virginia lawyer. In the aftermath of hot debate about Cook's efforts to employ blacks at the Portsmouth Navy Yard, Gardner attempted to use a cane on him, then tried to shoot him. Cook wrested the pistol from Gardner, shot him through the heart, and is reputed to have said: "Let him die there. I am satisfied."[59] The rules for dueling, if followed, were expected to produce more of the former attitude and less of the latter—more "honourable encounters" and fewer "barbaric outrages." This, at least, was the central defense for the rules and the activity they were established to govern.

[57] Kane, *Gentlemen, Swords and Pistols*, pp. 42–43; Howison, "Duelling in Virginia," p. 236.

[58] Gamble, *Savannah Duels*, p. 175.

[59] Howison, "Duelling in Virginia," pp. 240–244.

5

Dueling's Opponents

THUS far this discussion of dueling may have left the impression that there was no significant public opposition to the duel. Such an impression would be incorrect. Dueling and duelers had vigorous and vocal opponents, and the statute books of the several Southern states at various times throughout the colonial and antebellum years specified dueling as a crime. The problem was that public opinion generally refused to regard duelists as criminals, and this conflict between law and sentiment was not resolved until the duel, like many other Southern customs, became a casualty of the American Civil War.

Leadership of the antidueling forces came largely from newspaper editors and ministers. Of the two forces, newspaper editors may have had the greater effect. Newspapermen, as previously noted, were often principals on the field of honor—but despite that, or perhaps because of it, journalists fought the code with unabated fury. Witness, for example, the following editorial, which appeared in the Charleston, South Carolina, *City Gazette*:

> Departed this life, on Monday afternoon, Mr. Arthur Smith; and on Tuesday morning, Mr. Thomas Hutson—and yesterday, the remains of these young gentlemen were deposited in the tomb. . . . A challenge had been given and accepted—a duel was fought. . . . Such honor are thy triumphs! Come hither Duellist, and regale thy senses! See two young men . . . levelling the deadly tube at each other. . . . See them groaning on a deathbed; and now they breathe their last. Hear the distracted outcries of a fond and doting parent. . . . Oh thou idol, who delightest in human sacrifice; who snuffest up blood as sweet smelling

incense; when will thy reign case? Oh ye votaries of this Moloch, ye abetters of murder and bloodshed![1]

Other editors took up the hue and cry. An Alabama writer in 1828 noted: "[Duelists are] fireeaters and would-be gentlemen, who think it a greater disgrace to bear an imaginary insult than to murder a fellow-being in cold blood. . . . We would say that to all such testy touch-wood gentry, who are ready to draw a pistol if a cat should tread on their toe, the strong arm of the law should be applied."[2]

The editor of the Yorkville, South Carolina, *Compiler* in 1841 doubted that "the morals of the community . . . [are] so far gone, that it is necessary for a man to become his own avenger." As for the duelist, "if he falls, it should be without compassion; if he survives, it should be without respect."[3]

A Louisville, Kentucky, editor refused a challenge with this charge: "I look upon the miserable . . . code with a scorn equal to that which is getting to be felt for it by the whole civilized world of mankind." And a colleague of his in Knoxville, Kentucky, added, "I am opposed to duelling for the reason that it is contrary to the laws of my country, the law of humanity, and the law of God."[4]

The editor of the Charleston, South Carolina, *Observer* summed up the code of honor in these words: "Is it not rather a code of infamy, the very first principles of which every virtuous man must reprobate?" Noting an increase of duels in the 1830's, the same editor declared, "The spirit of murder is really in the community itself."[5]

[1] Charleston (S.C.) *City Gazette*, September 22, 1807.

[2] *Southern Advocate*, March 14, 1828.

[3] Yorkville (S.C.) *Compiler*, April 9, 1841.

[4] Kane, *Gentlemen, Swords and Pistols*, p. xiv; Seitz, *Famous Duels*, pp. 29–30.

[5] Charleston (S.C.) *Observer*, January 11, 1834, and March 17, 1838.

Perhaps the most active editor in antiduel work was F. W. Dawson of the Charleston, South Carolina, *News and Courier*. His editorials and stories, which included a scathing refusal of a challenge, won for him from Pope Leo XIII the title of "Knight of the Order of St. Gregory."[6]

Churchmen vied with journalists in condemning dueling and urging a cessation of the practice. Such a prominent minister as Arthur Wigfall of South Carolina publicly divorced the duelist from Christian fellowship. In a sermon preached in 1856, Wigfall said: "The code of Cain is but the original draft of the Code of Honor; their moral identity can not be mistaken. . . . The heathen, I tell you, are at your doors. . . . The Hindoo widow, who will perish upon the funeral pile of her husband sooner than endure scorn and lose her caste, is no whit more benighted than the pagan man of Honour, who seeks death sooner than endure the scoffs of public opinion."[7]

The famous Bishop Whipple in his diary declared that dueling was "contrary to the Christian religion," and the equally famed writer and traveling bookseller, "Parson" Mason Locke Weems, was author of a tract, *God's Revenge Against Duelling*.[8]

A South Carolina minister, Nathaniel Bowen, urged his congregation to strip from the duel "the respectability it has borrowed from illustrious names, and consign it to the contempt to which its origins, its principles, and its effects, so deservedly entitle it."[9]

---

[6] Columbus (Ohio) *Catholic Columbian*, December 17, 1904.

[7] Arthur Wigfall, *Sermon upon Duelling. Together with the Constitution of the Grahamville Association for the Suppression of Duelling* (Charleston: privately printed, 1856), p. 6.

[8] Whipple, *Southern Diary*, p. 115; Mason Locke Weems, *God's Revenge against Duelling* (Philadelphia, 1827).

[9] Nathaniel Bowen, *A Sermon; Preached October, 1807, in St. Michael's Church, Charleston* (Charleston: privately printed, 1823), p. 26.

The Reverend Timothy Dwight preached against dueling as early as 1805, but he was from New York and his printed sermon was probably not circulated in the South. Carolina minister William Barnwell was more likely to have had an impact. He catalogued dueling as "a barbarous practice . . . which provokes Jehovah, and defies his law; disturbs the state, and spurns its enactments; destroys men, and afflicts their families . . . [and] brings upon those that engage in it, certain misery both here and hereafter."[10]

Some of the powerful antiduel sermons came from men outside the ministerial and editorial professions, of course. One such speech was delivered in North Carolina shortly after the turn of the nineteenth century by a young legislator named Nash. It probably indicates more the status of the oratorical art in the pre–Civil War South than it does the strength of antidueling forces. Nash said, in part:

> We are told that the lofty spirit which leads the duellist to the field is one essential to the well-being of society— placing the weak upon a level with the strong, and redressing injuries which lie beyond the reach of the law—that if you could succeed in entirely abolishing the practice, you would introduce in its place assassination.
>
> Is this true, Sir? Do, indeed, the courtesies of life depend on the base principle of fear? . . . Is it, indeed, true, that we depend for any part of our comfort upon a practice condemned alike by the word of God and by the dictates of reason?

[10] William H. Barnwell, *The Impiety and Absurdity of Duelling: A Sermon* (Charleston: privately printed, 1844), pp. 5–6. The Reverend Dwight's tract is *A Sermon on Duelling* (New York: privately printed, 1905). Two additional printed sermons are J. R. Kendrick, *Duelling; A Sermon Preached at the First Baptist Church, Charleston, S.C., on Sunday Morning, August 7, 1853* (Charleston: privately printed, 1853), and Frederic Beasley, *A Sermon on Duelling, Delivered in Christ Church, Baltimore, April 28, 1811* (Baltimore: privately printed, 1811).

> No, Sir, the idea is not to be harbored. . . . What is that
> "lofty spirit" but the spirit of revenge and pride? Every
> virtuous feeling of the heart withers, every endearment is
> crushed and subdued. The desolating ruin the duellist is
> about to pour on others . . . cannot arrest his progress—
> he presses forward to his object regardless of every tie,
> social and divine, and glories in his laurels, though steeped
> in blood and bedewed with the tears of the widow and
> fatherless.[11]

Less emotional but perhaps more significant was the
baccalaureate address given by university president Phillip Lindsley in Nashville in 1827. He pointed out that the
dueling code had reached America from England. It was
strange, he said, that Southerners were so covetous of
what "savours of *high life*, that, without family, or estate,
or royal favour, or legal immunities" they had adopted
some of "the pompous phraseology and all the aristocratic
usages of that very country whose right to govern them
they have long since disclaimed and forever renounced."
This bald appeal to provincialism and old hatreds was
cunning, whether or not effective.[12]

In many towns, sermons, editorials, and speeches
were forerunners to the formation of antidueling societies. These organizations pledged themselves to try to
prevent all duels that came to their attention, and each
member bound himself to neither send nor accept a challenge. The Charleston Society, formed in 1826, carried on
its membership roster the names of several prominent
citizens and was led by General Charles Pinckney of Revolutionary War fame.[13]

An antidueling association was formed in Savannah
in 1826, with Dr. George Jones as its president. Dr. Jones
had been a member of Georgia's Constitutional Convention in 1798, and his name attracted other prominent citi-

---

[11] Gamble, *Savannah Duels*, pp. 300–301.

[12] Cited in Franklin, *Militant South*, p. 59.

[13] *Niles' Weekly Register* 31 (October 28, 1826), p. 131.

zens to association membership. The association had a standing committee of seven, which had the duty of preventing duels. Committee minutes indicate that it had some success. In 1836, for example, the following notice appears:

> The Standing Committee being informed some days since that a challenge to fight a Duel had been given by Mr. Thomas Bourke and accepted by Dr. Richard D. Arnold; after many fruitless personal efforts to reconcile the parties, resolved to address an official letter to the seconds, requesting their consent to entrust the affair to the decision of disinterested gentlemen, not members of the Association. This resolution was carried into effect, but did not answer the desired end. The committee then resolved to make one more effort to prevent A FASHIONABLE MURDER, and having obtained the co-operation of Messers. George Schley, W. T. Williams and James Hunter, again urged a reconciliation upon the seconds, who finally agreed to leave the matter with friends of their own selection. This was done, and the quarrel was settled in a manner honorable to both parties.[14]

Not all the antidueling societies, however, succeeded in their undertakings. In New Orleans, for instance, the society, begun by one hundred citizens in 1834, went out of business after some of the members reverted to previous habit and accepted challenges. Harriet Martineau remembered this New Orleans society in her volumes about America with these comments: "A Court of Honour was instituted [by the society] for the restraint of [dueling]; of course, without effectual result. Its function degenerated into choosing weapons for the combatants, so that it ended by sanctioning, instead of repressing, duelling."[15]

[14] Cited in Gamble, *Savannah Duels*, p. 199. See also pp. 185–200.

[15] Stuart Landry, *Duelling in Old New Orleans* (New Orleans: Pelican Publishing Co., 1950), pp. 20–22; Martineau, *Society in America*, 3:56.

Some opponents of dueling refused to have anything to do with the antidueling associations, believing them to be more social than serious and thus ineffective. In commenting on the organization of an association in Natchez, an editor wrote: "A very different remedy should be pursued. Let it be in all cases a crime of murder for one man to kill another in a duel, and let the law be rigidly executed in a few instances, and it will, in a short time, do more to suppress this odious practice than all the *Anti-Duelling Societies* that can be established from this time to the Millennium."[16]

Perhaps the editor was correct. The laws against dueling existed, in one form or another, but they were not "rigidly executed." Virginia had an antidueling law as early as 1776—a law carried forward as the commonwealth became a state—but it had no noteworthy deterring effect on duelists. Tennessee and North Carolina enacted no-duel laws in 1802, and Georgia's law was dated 1809. These laws, too, were ineffective.[17]

In South Carolina an antidueling act was fathered in 1812 by the great humanitarian Philip Moser—who was also author of one of the South's first laws making it murder to slay a black. Moser's dueling legislation provided that any party to a duel would be considered a felon and on conviction would be jailed for a year, made to pay a two-thousand-dollar fine, and forced to furnish bond as insurance for future good conduct. In addition, the act stated that a duelist would be barred from the ministry, law, medicine, or any public office. And, in a provision that was also a part of the Tennessee and North Carolina laws, the Moser act held that should a death result from a duel survivors could be tried for murder. The law was

---

[16] *Southern Advocate*, March 14, 1828.
[17] Howison, "Duelling in Virginia," pp. 221–222; Ashe, *North Carolina*, 2:185; Gamble, *Savannah Duels*, p. 131.

largely ignored. One man wrote, "that block-head Moser deserves to be gibbetted for his nonsensical law."[18]

Louisiana's antiduel law was enacted in 1818. Alabama and Mississippi passed laws in the 1830's. The District of Columbia forbade dueling in 1839, and a strongly worded Kentucky law was dated 1850. With the possible exception of the District of Columbia statute, none of them worked out very well. In the words of an able English observer, the antiduel laws were "no more than dead letters; the spirit of [American] institutions is adverse to such laws. . . ."[19]

Most of the no-duel laws contained provisions requiring an officeholder to take an oath that he had not been a duelist. The Alabama and Kentucky oaths were similar in this regard, stating in essence: "I have not fought a duel with a deadly weapon within this state or out of it with a citizen of this state." The Alabama oath then pledged the public official not to "give, accept, or knowingly carry a challenge . . . to any person or persons . . . to fight in single combat or otherwise, with any deadly weapon . . . or in any manner . . . aid or abet the same, during the time for which I am elected, or during my continuance in office, or during my continuance in the discharge of any public function."[20]

The ease with which these oaths were overcome is a commentary on the supremacy of unwritten law and class

---

[18] South Carolina, *Statutes at Large of South Carolina* (Columbia, 1836), 5:671–672; T. D. Jervey, *Robert Y. Hayne and His Times* (New York: Macmillan Co., 1909), pp. 197–198.

[19] U.S. Congress, Senate, *Congressional Globe*, 25th Cong., 2nd sess., March 2, 1838, p. 207; Louisiana, *Consolidation and Revision of the Statutes of the State* (New Orleans, 1852), p. 187; Alabama, *Digest of the Laws of the State of Alabama* (Philadelphia, 1833), p. 134; McLemore, *Mississippi*, pp. 296–297; Marryat, *Diary in America*, p. 161.

[20] Franklin, *Militant South*, p. 58; Seitz, *Famous Duels*, p. 29.

privilege in the Old South. By resolution, the 1841 Alabama General Assembly exempted thirteen citizens from taking the oath, and in 1848 it exempted five more. A special Mississippi resolution in 1838 allowed Henry Foote to skip the taking of the oath, and an Alabama act releasing William L. Yancey from the oath was passed over the governor's veto in 1846.[21]

Not only were the antiduel laws honored in the breach, but the toughest provisions of them suffered an inglorious fate when tested in court. Judges generally were reluctant to sustain laws that, they believed, might seriously infringe on the personal liberty of gentlemen. An illustration of this attitude is found in an 1819 South Carolina case, *The State* v. *John Edwards*. Edwards had been arrested for killing Dennis O'Driscoll in a duel. His became an early test case of all antidueling laws. Robert Y. Hayne, then the state's attorney general, prosecuted him with commendable zeal, but the case was lost when witnesses refused to testify on the ground their answers might be self-incriminatory. Once this point of view was upheld by the judge, the dueling laws became moot. "Duel this morning," wrote Charlestonian Jacob Schirmir in his journal; "Mr. L—— and Mr. D——. The former was instantly killed . . . he (D——) was indicted, but the grand jury ignored the bill."[22] Nonetheless, the antiduel movement remained alive. Inside the several legislatures, antiduel efforts continued. Some states passed addenda to existing laws, hoping thus to overcome judicial objections. South Carolina, for example, added to its law the statement that witnesses could legally be forced to give testimony with the pretrial understanding that such testimony

---

[21] Franklin, *Militant South*, pp. 60–61.

[22] *State* v. *John Edwards*, Nott & McCord, 2:13; Journal of Jacob Schirmir, August 2, 1853, South Carolina Historical Society, Charleston.

would not be used against them. Such efforts were of little value.[23]

In Tennessee an amended dueling act emphasized a provision that admission to the bar depended in part on the applicant's swearing a no-duel oath, for, one chronicler wrote, "it has been found [in Tennessee] that about ninety per cent of duels fought were between attorneys."[24]

The standard text in law during most of the antebellum years was Blackstone's *Commentaries*, and Blackstone recognized the problem of the duel in these words: "[for] deliberate duelling . . . the law has justly fixed the crime and punishment of murder. . . . Yet it requires such a degree of passive valor to combat the dread of even undeserved contempt arising from the false notions of honor . . . that the strongest prohibitions and penalties of the law will never be entirely effectual to eradicate this unhappy custom. . . ."[25]

Senator Lewis Linn of Missouri explained the issue in simpler language: "Duelling is like getting married," he wrote; "the more barriers erected against it, the surer are the interested parties to come together."[26]

The dueling laws did have some influence on the conduct of challenger and challenged. For one thing, many men chose to fight outside their home states. South Carolina courts attempted to stem this effort to evade their jurisdiction by handing down a split decision that duelists from inside the state were indictable, regardless of where they fought. But a substantial number of the gentry held faith in a thesis of full states' rights and believed that fighting duels just over the borders would exempt them from prosecution. Such reports as "they repaired across the North Carolina line and went for business"

---

[23] South Carolina, *Statutes of South Carolina*, 6:208, 515.
[24] Seitz, *Famous Duels*, p. 30.
[25] Cited in Howison, "Duelling in Virginia," p. 220.
[26] Cited in Kane, *Gentlemen, Swords and Pistols*, p. ix.

became commonplace, and some people believed that North and South Carolina had informal rules of accommodation allowing unhampered access and egress to each other's duelers.[27]

Men who came to Georgia from other states in order to fight duels made little effort to disguise the purpose of their visit. An Augusta newspaper, for example, noting that two South Carolinians had fought near that city, described the event as follows: "We had a show here two or three days ago. A party from Camden came here to fight a duel; and after preparing themselves, went to the ground at noon day through Broad street, with as much parade as if Lafayette had been coming. Carriages, gigs, sulkies and horsemen followed to witness the bloody deed. One of the combatants was killed instantly."[28]

Sam Houston's duel in Kentucky was an effort to avoid open violation of Tennessee law. On his return to Tennessee, authorities from Kentucky attempted unsuccessfully to extradite him.[29]

Duelists from the District of Columbia settled their difficulties at any of several places in Virginia and Maryland. A favorite site was Bladensburg Heights, located near Beltville. South Georgians used Amelia Island on the Florida side of the line, and Floridians came to Cumberland Island on the Georgia side. Tennessee and Louisiana duelists crossed to the western side of the Mississippi River for their affrays.[30]

Antidueling laws gave moral courage to some who,

[27] *State* v. *Walter Taylor*, South Carolina Reports, 1:107; Elizabeth Merritt, *James H. Hammond* (Baltimore: Johns Hopkins Press, 1923), p. 17.

[28] Cited in *Niles' Weekly Register* 35 (February 14, 1829): 405.

[29] Seitz, *Famous Duels*, p. 177.

[30] Ibid., p. 310; Howison, "Duelling in Virginia," pp. 225–227, 236; Whipple, *Southern Diary*, pp. 32–33; Hudson, *Humor in the Old South*, pp. 430–431.

once the duel had been declared a criminal act, felt justi-
fied in hailing slanderers and libelers to court rather than
to the field of honor. For instance, circuit court records
in eighteen of South Carolina's twenty-eight judicial dis-
tricts show only a single case of slander prior to 1812.
From 1812 to 1822, twenty-one such cases were heard,
and the increase was steady thereafter.[31]

The use of a legal weapon against loose talk and insult was an indicator as strong as any that the days of
the duel might be numbered. For instance, Southerner
Henry Willis violated the letter of the dueling code, but
expressed a new morality, when he wrote in 1824, "The
public are requested to suspend their opinions as respects
certain reports which have been industriously circulated,
injurious to my character. . . . I have directed a gentleman
of the Bar to commence an action against the author."[32]

"Acosta," one of the South's many nameless newspaper correspondents, was correct when he wrote in 1823
that he believed there might soon be a slowing of "licen-
tions of the *tongue,* of the *pen,* and of the *press.*" He believed this, he wrote, because the courts had begun to
"view this *satanic* evil" with a change in attitude. No
longer were cases being dismissed so quickly; indeed,
"large fines" were sometimes being levied by the judges.[33]
This judicial changestep was perhaps more valuable in
the long run than antidueling laws or antiduel societies
in reducing the number of appeals to the code of honor.

[31] See T. C. Bowen, "Crime and Punishment in South Carolina
prior to 1860" (M.A. thesis, University of South Carolina, 1929),
pp. 37–38.

[32] Charleston (S.C.) *Courier,* February 17, 1824.

[33] Yorkville (S.C.) *Pioneer,* November 1, 1823.

6

Persistence and Decline
of the Duel

DESPITE laws and courts and regardless of antiduel societies, dueling managed to thrive throughout the antebellum decades. This violent device could persist because the duel was an affair of class and caste, an important facet of Southern gentility and chivalric presumptions, a means by which Southern males could demonstrate their virility and prove their courage, and a mechanism for the protection of the nineteenth-century Southern man's most prized possession, his honor.

As pointed out in previous chapters, the formal duel was a part of the social training of upper-class Southern men, and the duel was nurtured and kept alive by these men. Dr. Marion Sims, one of the South's (and the nation's) greatest physicians in the 1800's, spoke for many of his social class when he wrote, late in his life, "I was educated to believe that duels inspired the proprieties of society. . . ." Another Southern gentleman remembered the duel as a code of procedure that "towers above the cloud of laws that blanket and hold in place the lower orders."[1]

To "hold in place the lower orders" was important to the Southern planter and to Southern gentlemen generally. Their slaveholding, highly class-conscious way of life depended on there being no revolution at the ballot

[1] E. L. Green, *History of the University of South Carolina* (Columbia: The State Company, 1916), p. 224; Lewis, "Dugger-Dromgoole Duel," pp. 344–345. See also Charles Sydnor, "The Southerner and the Laws," p. 17.

box or elsewhere and no strong questioning of the way things were. The South was a vast land area, thinly settled, and its planter aristocracy thrived on very large landholdings and very pronounced social prestige—the sort of prestige, in fact, that said to "King" Carter, who owned 300,000 acres and seven hundred slaves in Virginia, that when he arrived for church on Sunday morning the entire congregation would be waiting outside so that he might enter the sanctuary first—the sort of prestige that would be enhanced by a ritualistic expedient such as the duel.[2]

The cities and towns of the South were poorly developed and poorly policed. New Orleans, queen city of the gulf (sometimes called the Southern Babylon), had open gutters used for sewers until 1857. Mobile, Macon, and Richmond had a dearth of paved streets, and residents of these towns alternated in breathing thick dust and wading through thick mud. Charleston and Savannah were richest and most progressive—but they, too, were undistinguished by comparison with northern or foreign centers. Charleston's buildings were remembered by one visitor as "singularly mean, and many of them such as would be thought shabby in an ordinary Scotch village." Englishman George Featherstonhaugh remembered all Southern towns as having "one endless street . . . crowded with men all upon a level in greediness and vulgarity. . . ." In such an environment, the less-favored congregated and were inclined to rowdyism and worse. In their brawling with one another, they might "scratch, bite and gouge, bite fingers, nose, ears, gouge out eyes, blate like goats" —but they had respect, apparently, for the gentleman class.[3]

[2] Eaton, *Freedom of Thought*, p. 3.

[3] Stirling, *Letters from the Slave States*, p. 250; George W. Featherstonhaugh, *Excursion through the Slave States from Wash-*

Faced with a social structure that included not only these rough whites but also free blacks and black slaves, the ruling class established something of a feudal regime, an Old World aristocracy in a New World wilderness. Such an aristocracy gave its leading citizens a station in life both comfortable and much priviliged. They would dominate the three branches of government, command the police and militia (jealously guarding their titles of rank), and have separate rules (unwritten more than written) for their personal conduct, business and social.

This modified aristocracy was supported no less by the ruling class than by the middle group of shopkeepers, small farmers, and other poor but bright men who could see the possibility of someday joining the top rank. Nationally prominent John C. Calhoun had made the great jump. So had editor J. D. B. De Bow, bank president Langdon Cheves, and poet, college teacher, and wealthy lawyer Mitchell King.[4]

The formal duel fit easily and well into this concept of aristocracy. The duel, as a means of settling disputes, could be restricted to use by the upper class. Dueling would demonstrate uncompromising courage, stability, calmness under stress, gentility, and chivalric superiority. In the South, as in England and France in earlier years, the duel would be considered a hallmark of refinement in man's relationship to his fellowman.

The duel also would demonstrate to all the raw courage and undoubted masculinity of the gentry. The possession of these qualities—courage and maleness—was absolutely essential to the Southern gentleman, not only to the preservation of his system of class superiority but

ington on the Potomac to the Frontier of Mexico, 2 vols. (London: John Murray, 1844), 2:329–330; Wade, *Longstreet*, p. 173.

[4] Eaton, *Growth of Southern Civilization*, p. 21. On this general topic, see also pp. 1–24, 150–176, 295–324; Franklin, *Militant South*, pp. 2–79.

to his acceptance by his peers.

Indeed, the fear of being branded a coward was a powerful phobia. Fathers preached courage and manliness to their sons, urging them to forego such effeminate pastimes as playing the piano and to devote their time to "manly training." An English observer reported a more serious aspect of this father-son relationship when he wrote in 1837: "I recollect a gentleman introducing me to the son of another gentleman who was present. The lad, who was about fourteen, I should think, shortly after left the room; and then the gentleman told me, before the boy's father, that the lad was one of the right sort, having already fought and wounded his man; and the father smiled complacently at this tribute to the character of his son."[5]

Even writing was considered by some to be less than manly. John Esten Cooke, for instance, asked his publisher not to identify him as the author of a popular novel, *Leatherstocking and Silk*. "Being identified as the writer . . . would materially injure me I fear in my profession," he explained.[6]

Any man in the South who left the slightest doubt as to his willingness to engage in male rough-and-tumble or to fight for his state or country could be the target of much abuse. He might be the object of posters announcing his shortcoming ("We pronounce WILLIAM PLOUDEN a COWARD"), or he might be sent various reminders of his faintheartedness. Henry Stanley, who had moved to Arkansas from England, neglected to volunteer promptly for the Confederate army. He then received in the mail a parcel of women's undergarments. Without further delay, he joined a local regiment.[7]

[5] Cited in Eaton, *Growth of Southern Civilization*, p. 321; Marryat, *Diary in America*, p. 161.

[6] Eaton, *Growth of Southern Civilization*, p. 321.

[7] Stanley, *Autobiography*, p. 157.

A Mississippi leader thought to be a coward was burned in effigy, then posted in a local newspaper with this verse:

> Alas! Let this hereafter be
> A warning to the rest
> We love a brave and valiant man
> A coward we detest.[8]

Indeed, a coward was detested. One writer stated that anyone who refused a fight "would never again be permitted to join gentlemen even in a fox hunt. He's utterly out of it." Another observer wrote that "a man could no more decline to fight a duel than a woman could compromise her virtue without exciting the contempt of society."[9]

For the "crackers," "peckerwoods," "piney woods folk" (the poor whites), the periodic proving of virility took the form of brawling in the streets or at taverns or feuding at militia musters—"cursing, biting . . . and, after victory, jumping upon a stump and crowing like a cock." For the gentleman class there was the hunt (after the fox, over the meanest terrain, personal danger of no concern), the ring tournament (snaring small rings with a long lance from horseback at full gallop), the riding of night patrol to frustrate crimes and slave escapes, perhaps to nip a black rebellion in the bud—and, above all else, there was the duel, the bloody code, the going to the iron man.

One Southern historian defines the duel as "a shield of personal honor," and perhaps he is correct. At any rate, to the antebellum Southern gentleman it was that. And being that, it was intensely significant. For a Southerner, personal honor, while an intangible concept, was no

---

[8] Cited in Franklin, *Militant South*, p. 8.

[9] Sydnor, "The Southerner and the Laws," p. 18; Srygley, *Seventy Years in Dixie*, p. 309.

less real than any physical possession and among these possessions no less valuable than the most expensive and cherished. And if there were undesirable aspects of dueling—i.e., death—nonetheless, one Southerner argued, "a custom recognized by [Southern gentlemen] to keep the world pliant to the touch of honor cannot be all bad."[10]

To the Southern gentleman, honor had many facets. A gentleman paid his debts or made prompt arrangement about them. His word was always his bond, and no contracts were necessary in relationships with him. He was truthful, patriotic, courageous.

Honor meant that a Southern gentleman was courtly and deferential in his association with women. The marriage tie was respected; there was to be praise for female chastity; there was to be an exaggerated modesty of language when women were present—all this applicable, of course, primarily to women of the upper classes. Honor meant that no woman—no gentlewoman—should be embarrassed or insulted. Certainly no female member of a man's family, whatever the degree of consanguinity, was to be considered as having any but the loftiest qualities of character. Any imputation to the contrary was an assault, to be fiercely combated on the field of honor. One Southerner wrote that a gentleman "must be willing to risk life itself in defense of his own good name and that of a member of his family."[11]

The perception of honor meant that every gentleman was responsible for the defense of his own. Neither police nor court of law should be called to do for a man what the code dictated he do for himself. Thus, honor discouraged

[10] Rosser H. Taylor, *Ante-Bellum South Carolina* (Chapel Hill: University of North Carolina Press, 1942), p. 47; Lewis, "Dugger-Dromgoole Duel," p. 345.

[11] Lewis, "Dugger-Dromgoole Duel," p. 344. On the status of women, see Eaton, *Growth of Southern Civilization*, p. 13; and Eaton, *Freedom of Thought*, pp. 52–53.

the growth of strong law enforcement agencies in the South and lessened the effectiveness of the state courts.

Honor as an ideal extended in scope to cover numerous activities in various walks of life. Should a question arise as to whether honor was involved, the answer, to be on the safe side, was generally affirmative. "Their code of honour," traveller Alexander Mackay wrote of Virginians, "is so exceedingly strict that it requires the greatest circumspection to escape its violation."[12] His observation applied equally to all Southern states.

So it was that the notion of honor caused duels and was perhaps the single most telling force in the persistence of the duel throughout the pre–Civil War years of the nineteenth century. With regard to his honor, however loosely defined, the Southern gentleman adopted the philosophy of a nameless Georgia poet who wrote:

> Set honor in one eye, and death in the other,
> And I will look on both indifferently:
> For, let the gods so speed me as I love
> The name of honor more than I fear death.[13]

Perhaps the brave, generous notions of honor and chivalry remained alive to some extent after the 1860's, but the duel did not. Formal dueling, in fact, steadily declined, especially after the election of Andrew Jackson (great dueler that he was) heralded the downfall of class consciousness as a viable force. The duel lost favor at about the same time and with about the same rate of decline as did the influence of the planter class generally.

Great winds of change swept through the South from the mid-1830's forward, and particularly after the Mexi-

---

[12] Mackay, *The Western World*, 1:254.

[13] Cited in Gamble, *Savannah Duels*, p. 302. On the concept of honor, see also Wilbur J. Cash, *The Mind of the South* (New York: A. A. Knopf, 1941), pp. 30–35; Rollin J. Osterweis, *Romanticism and Nationalism in the Old South* (New Haven: Yale University Press, 1949), pp. 82–102.

can-American War in 1845. An emphasis on industry was apparent, and a new industrial spirit was noticable. Mills and factories of various sorts appeared on the Southern landscape. Men talked profit and loss and argued the merits of free-white labor over slave labor. The lure of the frontier was strong, and planters in increasing numbers left their worn-out lands for fresh acres in Texas, California, Oregon—the new El Dorado of America. As these planters left the Old South, they weakened the aristocratic structure and reduced the effect of planter-inspired law and custom.

Transportation advances (especially the spread of railways) lessened the isolation of Southerners one from another and of all from the rest of America. National patterns of thought became better known, and Northern styles in dress, social conduct, amusement, and politics became less a matter of mystery.

The untitled people of the South became restless as the antebellum years passed, less satisfied with the status quo, more willing to speak out—a noteworthy departure from the climate of opinion required for the maintenance of a ruling aristocracy. In 1844, for instance, the slaveless farmers of low-country South Carolina openly rebelled against the domination of the state legislature by slave owners. Earlier, the planters in Alabama had begun to lose political control. And in 1846 a mechanic was the candidate for mayor of Charleston. His backers urged his election on a class basis. "Will you suffer your brother to be trampled on," they wrote, "by the silk stocking gentry, who wish to have a *gentleman* in office?"[14]

[14] Charleston (S.C.) *Mercury*, September 5, 1846. On the decline of the planter aristocracy, see Clanton Williams, "Early Ante-Bellum Montgomery: A Black Belt Constituency," *Journal of Southern History* 7 (1941): 495–525, especially p. 522; Eaton, *Freedom of Thought*, pp. 84–88; Fletcher Green, *Constitutional Development in the South Atlantic States, 1776–1860* (Chapel Hill: University of North Carolina Press, 1930), chap. 7.

All this discontent was mild by current standards of political and social protest, but it served nonetheless to weaken the posture of the planter class as leaders of Southern thought and economy. The duel was a victim of this political and philosophic struggle, for as the planters lost their hold they gave ground. And as the children of planters replaced their fathers as family heads, they moved with even more speed away from concepts and customs such as the duel, which seemed of little practical value if not outright archaic.

Some regretted the passing of the old ways, but they were powerless to prevent it. One aristocratic planter complained:

> But now the silver-mounted, smooth bore duelling pistols have given away to the rifled barreled revolvers, and quick snap shooting on the street [has] superseded the old fashioned ten paces. . . . The formality of a challenge is now out of fashion and the hip pocket is now inserted in every man's trousers. Both methods are barbarous, but I am inclined to think that the old time method was the least so, as it gave one time to make his will and hope for an apology.[15]

More and more with each passing year, though, the duel gained a reputation as being closer kin to manslaughter and murder than to a medieval tournament or an "aesthetic mode of settling difficulties."[16] Economic modernization and population diversity in the South were increasingly antagonistic to the stability of landed gentry. A spreading democratism dictated an end to a code of behavior which called for disobedience to law along class lines.

At the apex of all this was the Civil War. It is axiom-

---

[15] Arney Childs, ed., *Rice Planter and Sportsman: The Recollections of J. Motte Alston, 1821–1907* (Columbia: University of South Carolina Press, 1953), p. 21.
[16] Ibid.

atic that a major war in a nation leaves in its wake certain and lasting changes to many of the country's customs and mores, its concepts of morality, its reverence for tradition, and its system of interpersonal relationships. The Civil War, certainly, brought such alterations to the American South. Whatever changes were being made were expedited by the war, and in the bitterness of defeat Southern men shook free of such symbolic customs as the duel. After 1865 duels were as rare as they had previously been numerous. The "bottom rail was now on top," and social status no longer served as an excuse for breach of the law. Further, a citizen who had fought his way through four years of devastating fratricidal warfare had little concern about being called a coward.

In sum, the postwar years were too filled with efforts to rebuild from the ruins to allow the luxury of a return to romanticized chivalry. Aristocrats were now at work with their hands. In the words of New-South orator Henry Grady, the planter had returned to "find his home in ruins, his farm devastated, his slaves free, his stock killed, his barns empty, his trade destroyed, his money worthless . . . his comrades slain, and the burden of others heavy on his shoulders." Humorist-philosopher Bill Arp (Charles Henry Smith) of Kentucky and Georgia expressed it in different language. "The war had bekum mity hevy on us," he wrote, "and atter the big kollapse we . . . was a strugglin to rise from out the reck, to breethe the air above us, to take a invoise and see if there was enuf to live for. . . ." Southerners had decided to make a little money to go along with their honor, he said, for some of the former was necessary to keep the latter from "degeneratin."[17] The duel had no place in such a setting. Indeed, some of the survivors of the giant war must have

[17] Jack K. Williams, "Three Georgians on Sectional Reconciliation," *Emory University Quarterly* 7 (1951) : 223, 221.

wondered if acceptance of the code of honor was not in part an explanation of the personality of those who had led the South into the gigantic four-year mass duel that had given it such grievous wounds.

In 1872 James Southall, editor of the Richmond, Virginia, *Enquirer*, and Alexander Moseley, editor of the Richmond *Whig*, went through the formalities of the pre-challenge and challenge. Both men were forthwith arrested and forced to post heavy bail. They decided not to continue the duel.

In the summer of 1877 two young Savannah lawyers met for a duel. Various difficulties beset their efforts to shoot each other. First, they lost their way to the secret meeting place. Second, following a harmless exchange of shots, dusk fell, making it difficult to aim. Third, one second announced that his man was nearsighted and would require special dispensation. Suddenly it seemed that some solution other than shooting should be found. An agreement was reached to forget the original disagreement. All went home, the two principals became fast friends, and Savannah's last duel became historical record.

In 1880, Colonel E. B. C. Cash of Darlington County, South Carolina, fought and killed William Shannon in a duel. Cash was arrested and tried for murder. Although acquitted on a technicality, he was widely considered a murderer thereafter and spent much of his life writing defenses to justify his action.

In 1883, Richard Bierne and William Elam fought a duel near Waynesboro, Virginia. Elam was wounded. Police set out to arrest Bierne, who was forced to leave the state.[18]

Clearly, dueling was no longer acceptable to the peo-

[18] Seitz, *Famous Duels*, p. 32; Hudson, *Journalism in America*, p. 278; Gamble, *Savannah Duels*, pp. 298–300; E. B. C. Cash, *The Cash-Shannon Duel* (Greenville, S.C.: privately printed, 1881); Kane, *Gentlemen, Swords and Pistols*, pp. 257–269.

ple, gentry or otherwise, as a reasonable method for revenge. Opinion had at last crystallized, and when that happened the unwritten law gave way to the written and the code of honor died a less than honorable death.

THE CODE OF HONOR

THE

CODE OF HONOR

OR,

RULES FOR THE GOVERNMENT

OF

PRINCIPALS AND SECONDS

IN

DUELLING.

BY JOHN LYDE WILSON,

EX-GOVERNOR OF SOUTH CAROLINA.

CHARLESTON:

1838.

TO THE PUBLIC.

———

THE man who adds in any way to the sum of human happiness
is strictly in the discharge of a moral duty. When Howard visited the victims of crime and licentiousness, to reform their
habits and ameliorate their condition, the question was never
asked whether he had been guilty of like excesses or not? The
only question the philanthropist would propound, should be, has
the deed been done in the true spirit of Christian benevolence?
Those who know me, can well attest the motive which has
caused the publication of the following sheets, to which they
for a long time urged me in vain. Those who do not know me
have no right to impute a wrong motive; and if they do, I had
rather be the object than the authors of condemnation. To pub-
lish a CODE OF HONOR, to govern in cases of individual combat,
might seem to imply, that the publisher was an advocate of
duelling and wished to introduce it as the proper mode of de-
ciding all personal difficulties and misunderstandings. Such im-
plication would do me great injustice. But if the question be
directly put to me, whether there are not cases where duels are
right and proper, I would unhesitatingly answer, there are. If
an oppressed nation has a right to appeal to arms in defence of
its liberty and the happiness of its people, there can be no argument used in support of such appeal, which will not apply with
equal force to individuals. How many cases are there, that
might be enumerated, where there is no tribunal to do justice
to an oppressed and deeply wronged individual? If he be sub-
jected to a tame submission to insult and disgrace, where no
power can shield him from its effects, then indeed it would
seem, that the first law of nature, self preservation, points out
the only remedy for his wrongs. The history of all animated
nature exhibits a determined resistance to encroachments upon
natural rights—nay, I might add, inanimate nature, for it also
exhibits a continual warfare for supremacy. Plants of the same
kind, as well as trees, do not stop their vigorous growth be-

cause they overshadow their kind; but on the contrary, flourish
with greater vigor as the more weak and delicate decline and
die. Those of different species are at perpetual warfare. The
sweetest rose tree will sicken and waste away on the near approach of the noxious bramble, and the most promising fields
of wheat yield a miserable harvest if choked up with tares and
thistles. The elements themselves war together, and the angels
of heaven have met in fierce encounter. The principle of self-
preservation is co-extensive with creation; and when by education we make character and moral worth a part of ourselves,
we guard these possessions with more watchful zeal than life
itself, and would go farther for their protection. When one
finds himself avoided in society, his friends shunning his approach, his substance wasting, his wife and children in want
around him, and traces all his misfortune and misery to the
slanderous tongue of the calumniator, who, by secret whisper
or artful inuendo, had sapped and undermined his reputation,
he must be more or less than man to submit in silence.

The indiscriminate and frequent appeal to arms, to settle
trivial disputes and misunderstandings, cannot be too severely
censured and deprecated. I am no advocate for such duelling.
But in cases where the laws of the country give no redress for
injuries received, where public opinion not only authorizes but
enjoins resistance, it is needless and a waste of time to denounce the practice. It will be persisted in as long as a manly
independence and a lofty personal pride, in all that dignifies
and ennobles the human character, shall continue to exist. If a
man be smote on one cheek in public, and he turns the other,
which is also smitten, and he offers no resistance, but blesses
him that so despitefully used him, I am aware he is in the exercise of great Christian forbearance, highly recommended and
enjoined by many very good men, but utterly repugnant to
those feelings which nature and education have implanted in
the human character. If it was possible to enact laws so severe
and impossible to be evaded, as to enforce such a rule of behavior, all that is honorable in the community would quit the
country, and inhabit the wilderness with the Indians. If such
a course of conduct was infused by education into the minds of
our youth, and it became praise-worthy and honorable to a man
to submit to insult and indignity, then indeed the forbearance
might be borne without disgrace. Those, therefore, who condemn all, who do not denounce duelling in every case, should

establish schools where a passive submission to force would be the exercise of a commendable virtue. I have not the least doubt if I had been educated in such a school, and lived in such a society, I would have proved a very good member of it. But I very much doubt, if a seminary of learning was established, where this Christian forbearance was inculcated and enforced, whether there would be many scholars.

I would not wish to be understood to say that I do not desire to see duelling cease to exist entirely, in society. But my plan for doing it away, is essentially different from the one which teaches a passive forbearance to insult and indignity.— I would inculcate in the rising generation a spirit of lofty independence; I would have them taught that nothing was more derogatory to the honor of a gentleman than to wound the feelings of anyone, however humble. That if wrong be done to another, it was more an act of heroism and bravery to repair the injury, than to persist in error, and enter into mortal combat with the injured party. That this would be an aggravation of that which was already odious, and would put him without the pale of all decent society and honorable men. I would strongly inculcate the propriety of being tender of the feelings as well as the failings of those around him. I would teach immutable integrity, and uniform urbanity of manners. Scrupulously to guard individual honor, by a high personal self-respect, and the practice of every commendable virtue. Once let such a system of education be universal, and we should seldom hear, if ever, of any more duelling.

The severest penal enactments cannot restrain the practice of duelling, and their extreme severity in this State, the more effectually shields the offender. The teaching and preaching of our eloquent clergy may do some service, but is wholly inadequate to suppress it. Under these circumstances, the following rules are given to the public, and if I can save the life of one useful member of society, I will be compensated.—I have restored to the bosom of many, their sons, by my timely interference, who are ignorant of the misery I have averted from them. I believe that nine duels out of ten, if not ninety-nine out of a hundred, originate in the want of experience in the seconds. A book of authority, to which they can refer in matters where they are uninformed, will therefore be *desideratum*. How far this Code will be that book, the public must decide.

THE AUTHOR.

CHAPTER I.

THE PERSON INSULTED, BEFORE CHALLENGE SENT.

1. Whenever you believe you are insulted, if the insult be in public, and by words or behavior, never resent it there, if you have self-command enough to avoid noticing it. If resented there, you offer an indignity to the company, which you should not.

2. If the insult be by blows or any personal indignity, it may be resented at the moment, for the insult to the company did not originate with you. But although resented at the moment, yet you are bound still to have satisfaction, and must therefore make the demand.

3. When you believe yourself aggrieved, be silent on the subject, speak to no one about the matter, and see your friend who is to act for you, as soon as possible.

4. Never send a challenge in the first instance, for that precludes all negotiation. Let your note be in the language of a gentleman, and let the subject matter of complaint be truly and fairly set forth, cautiously avoiding attributing to the adverse party any improper motive.

5. When your second is in full possession of the facts, leave the whole matter to his judgment, and avoid any consultation with him unless he seeks it. He has the custody of your honor, and by obeying him you cannot be compromitted.

6. Let the time of demand upon your adversary after the insult be as short as possible, for he has the right to double that time in replying to you, unless you give some good reason for your delay. Each party is entitled to reasonable time to make the necessary domestic arrangements, by will or otherwise before fighting.

7. To a written communication you are entitled to a written reply, and it is the business of your friend to require it.

SECOND'S DUTY BEFORE CHALLENGE SENT.

1. Whenever you are applied to by a friend to act as his second, before you agree to do so, state distinctly to your principal that you will be governed only by your own judgment, that *he* will not be consulted after you are in full possession of the facts, unless it becomes necessary to make or accept the *amende* honorable, or send a challenge. You are supposed to be cool and collected, and your friend's feelings are more or less irritated.

2. Use every effort to soothe and tranquilize your principal, do not see things in the same aggravated light in which he views them, extenuate the conduct of his adversary whenever you see clearly an opportunity to do so, without doing violence to your friend's irritated mind. Endeavor to persuade him that there must have been some misunderstanding in the matter. Check him if he uses opprobrious epithets towards his adversary, and never permit improper or insulting words in the note you carry.

3. To the note you carry in writing to the party complained of, you are entitled to a written answer, which will be directed to your principal, and will be delivered to you by his adversary's friend. If this note be not written in the style of a gentleman, refuse to receive it, and assign your reason for such refusal. If there be a question made as to the character of the note, require the second presenting it to you, who considers it respectful, to endorse upon it these words: "I consider the note of my friend respectful, and would not have been the bearer of it, if I believed otherwise."

4. If the party called on refuses to receive the note you bear, you are entitled to demand a reason for such refusal.— If he refuses to give you any reason, and persists in such refusal, he treats, not only your friend, but yourself with indignity, and you must then make yourself the actor, by sending a respectful note, requiring a proper explanation of the course he has pursued towards you and your friend; and if he still adheres to his determination, you are to challenge or post him.

5. If the person to whom you deliver the note of your friend declines meeting him, on the ground of inequality, you are bound to tender yourself in his stead, by a note directed to him from yourself, and if he refuses to meet you, you are to post him.

6. In all cases of the substitution of the second for the

principal, the seconds should interpose and adjust the matter, if the party substituting avows he does not make the quarrel of his principal his own. The true reason of substitution, is the supposed insult of imputing to you the like inequality which is charged upon your friend, and when the contrary is declared, there should be no fight, for individuals may well differ in their estimate of an individual's character and standing in society. In case of substitution and a satisfactory arrangement, you are then to inform your friend of all the facts, whose duty it will be to post in person.

7. If the party, to whom you present a note, employ a son, father or brother as a second, you must decline acting with either, on the ground of consanguinity.

8. If a minor wishes you to take a note to an adult, decline doing so on the ground of his minority. But if the adult complained of, had made a companion of the minor in society, you may bear the note.

9. When an accommodation is tendered, never require too much; and if the party offering the *amende* honorable wishes to give a reason for his conduct in the matter, do not, unless offensive to your friend, refuse to receive it; by so doing, you heal the breach more effectually.

10. If a stranger wish you to bear a note for him, be well satisfied before you do so, that he is on an equality with you; and in presenting the note, state to the party the relationship you stand towards him, and what you know and believe about him; for strangers are entitled to redress for wrongs as well as others, and the rules of honor and hospitality should protect them.

CHAPTER II.

THE PARTY RECEIVING A NOTE BEFORE CHALLENGE.

1. When a note is presented to you by an equal, receive it, and read it, although you may suppose it to be from one you do not intend to meet, because its requisites may be of a character which may be readily complied with. But if the requirements of the note cannot be acceded to, return it through the medium of your friend to the person who handed it to you, with your reason for returning it.

2. If the note received be in abusive terms, object to its reception and return it for that reason, but if it be respectful, return an answer of the same character, in which respond correctly and openly to all interrogatories fairly propounded, and hand it to your friend, who it is presumed you have consulted, and who has advised the answer; direct to the opposite party, and let it be delivered to his friend.

3. You may refuse to receive a note from a minor, if you have not made an associate of him, one that has been posted, one that has been publicly disgraced without resenting it, one whose occupation is unlawful, a man in his dotage and a lunatic. There may be other cases, but the character of those enumerated will lead to a correct decision upon those omitted.

If you receive a note from a stranger, you have a right to a reasonable time to ascertain his standing in society, unless he be fully vouched for, by his friend.

4. If a party delays calling on you for a week or more after the supposed insult, and assigns no cause for the delay, if you require it, you may double the time before you respond to him; for the wrong cannot be considered aggravated if borne patiently for same days, and the time may have been used in preparation and practice.

SECOND'S DUTY OF THE PARTY RECEIVING A NOTE BEFORE CHALLENGE SENT.

1. When consulted by your friend who has received a note requiring explanation, inform him distinctly that he must be governed wholly by you in the progress of the dispute. If he refuse, decline to act on that ground.

2. Use your utmost efforts to allay all excitement which your principal may labor under; search diligently into the origin of the misunderstanding; for gentlemen seldom insult each

other, unless they labor under some misapprehension or mistake; and when you have discovered the original ground of error, follow each movement to the time of sending the note, and harmony will be restored.

3. When your principal refuses to do what you require of him, decline further acting on that ground, and inform the opposing second of your withdrawal from the negotiation.

CHAPTER III.

DUTY OF CHALLENGEE AND HIS SECOND BEFORE FIGHTING.

1. After all efforts for a reconciliation are over, the party aggrieved sends a challenge to his adversary, which is delivered to his second.

2. Upon the acceptance of the challenge, the seconds make the necessary arrangements for the meeting, in which each party is entitled to a perfect equality. The old notion that the party challenged was authorized to name the time, place, distance and weapon, has been long since exploded, nor would a man of chivalric honor use such a right if he possessed it. The time must be as soon as practicable, the place such as had ordinarily been used where the parties are, the distance usual, and the weapon that which is most generally used, which in this State is the pistol.

3. If the challenger insist upon what is not usual in time, place, distance and weapon, do not yield the point, and tender in writing what is usual in each, and if he refuse to give satisfaction, then your friend may post him.

4. If your friend be determined to fight and not post, you have the right to withdraw. But if you continue to act, and the challengee name a distance and weapon not usual and more fatal than the ordinary distance and weapon, you have the right to tender a still more deadly distance and weapon, and he must accept.

5. The usual distance is from ten to twenty paces, as may be agreed on, and the seconds in measuring the ground usually step three feet.

6. After all the arrangements are made, the seconds determine the giving of the word and position by lot, and he who gains has the choice of the one or the other, selects whether it

be the word or position, but he cannot have both.

———

CHAPTER IV.

DUTY OF CHALLENGEE AND SECOND AFTER CHALLENGE SENT.

1. The challengee has not option when negotiation has ceased but to accept the challenge.

2. The second makes the necessary arrangements with the second of the person challenged. The arrangements are detailed in the preceding chapter.

———

CHAPTER V.

DUTIES OF PRINCIPALS AND SECONDS ON THE GROUND.

1. The principals are to be respectful in meeting, and neither by look or expression irritate each other. They are to be wholly passive, being entirely under the guidance of their seconds.

2. When once posted, they are not to quit their positions under any circumstances, without the leave or direction of their second.

3. When the principals are posted, the second giving the word, must tell them to stand firm until he repeats the giving of the word, in the manner it will be given when the parties are at liberty to fire.

4. Each second has a loaded pistol, in order to enforce a fair combat according to the rules agreed on; and if a principal fires before the word or time agreed on, he is at liberty to fire at him, and if such second's principal fall, it is his duty to do so.

5. If after a fire either party be touched, the duel is to end; and no second is excusable who permits a wounded friend to fight, nor no second who knows his duty will permit his friend to fight a man already hit. I am aware there have been many instances where a contest has continued, not only after slight, but severe wounds had been received. In all such cases I think the seconds are blameable.

6. If after an exchange of shots, neither party is hit, it is the duty of the second of the challengee to approach the second

of the challenger and say: "Our friends have exchanged shots, are you satisfied, or is there any cause why the contest should be continued?" If the meeting be of no serious cause of complaint, where the party complaining had in no way been deeply injured, or grossly insulted, the second of the party challenging should reply: "The point of honor being settled, there can, I conceive, be no objection to a reconciliation, and I propose that our principals meet on middle ground, shake hands and be friends." If this be acceded to by the second of the challengee, the second of the party challenging says: "We have agreed that the present duel shall cease—the honor of each of you is preserved, and you will meet on middle ground, shake hands and be reconciled."

7. If the insult be of serious character, it will be the duty of the second of the challenger to say in reply to the second of the challengee: "We have been deeply wronged, and if you are not disposed to repair the injury, the contest must continue." And if the second of the challengee offers nothing by way of reparation, the fight continues until one or the other of the principals is hit.

8. If in cases where the contest is ended by the seconds, as mentioned in the sixth rule of this chapter, the parties refuse to meet and be reconciled, it is the duty of the seconds to withdraw from the field, informing their principals that the contest must be continued under the superintendence of other friends. But if one agrees to this arrangement of the seconds and the other does not, the second of the disagreeing principal only withdraws.

9. If either principal on the ground refuse to fight, or continue the fight when required, it is the duty of his second to say to the other second: "I have come upon the ground with a coward, and have to tender you my apology for an ignorance of his character; you are at liberty to post him." The second, by such conduct, stands excused to the opposite party.

10. When the duel is ended by a party being hit, it is the duty of the second to the party so hit, to announce the fact to the second of the party hitting, who will forthwith tender any assistance he can command to the disabled principal.—If the party challenging hit the challengee, it is his duty to say he is satisfied, and will leave the ground. If the challenger be hit, upon the challengee being informed of it, he should ask, through his second, whether he was at liberty to leave the ground, which should be assented to.

CHAPTER VI.

WHO SHOULD BE ON THE GROUND.

1. The principals, seconds, and one surgeon and one assistant surgeon to each principal, but the assistant surgeon may be dispensed with.

2. Any number of friends that the seconds agree on, may be present, provided they do not come within the degrees of consanguinity mentioned in the seventh rule of Chapter 1.

3. Persons admitted on the ground are carefully to abstain by word or behaviour, from any act that might be the least exceptionable, nor should they stand near the principals or seconds, or hold conversations with them.

CHAPTER VII.

ARMS, AND MANNER OF LOADING AND PRESENTING THEM.

1. The arms used should be smooth-bore pistols, not exceeding nine inches in length, with flint and steel. Percussion pistols may be mutually used if agreed on, but to object on that account is lawful.

2. Each second informs the other when he is about to load and invites his presence, but the seconds rarely attend on such invitation, as gentlemen may be safely trusted in the matter.

3. The second in presenting the pistol to his friend, should never put it in his pistol hand, but should place it in the other, which is grasped midway the barrel, with the muzzle pointing in the contrary way to that which he is to fire, informing him that his pistol is loaded and ready for use. Before the word is given, the principal grasps the butt firmly in his pistol hand, and brings it round, with the muzzle downward, to the fighting position.

4. The fighting position is with the muzzle down and the barrel from you, for although it may be agreed that you may hold your pistols with the muzzle up, it may be objected to, as you can fire sooner from that position, and consequently have a decided advantage, which ought not to be claimed, and should not be granted.

CHAPTER VIII.

THE DEGREES OF INSULT, AND HOW COMPROMISED.

1. The prevailing rule is, that words used in retort, although more violent and disrespectful than those first used, will not satisfy—words being no satisfaction for words.

2. When words are used, and a blow given in return, the insult is avenged, and if redress be sought, it must be from the person receiving the blow.

3. When blows are given in the first instance and returned, and the person first striking be badly beaten or otherwise, the party first struck is to make the demand, for blows do not satisfy a blow.

4. Insults at a wine table, when the company are overexcited, must be answered for; and if the party insulting have no recollection of the insult, it is his duty to say so in writing, and negative the insult. For instance, if a man say, "you are a liar and no gentleman," he must, in addition to the plea of the want of recollection, say: "I believe the party insulted to be a man of the strictest veracity and a gentleman."

5. Intoxication is not a full excuse for insult, but it will greatly palliate. If it was a full excuse, it might well be counterfeited to wound feelings, or destroy character.

6. In all cases of intoxication, the seconds must use a sound discretion under the above general rules.

7. Can every insult be compromised? is a mooted and vexed question. On this subject no rules can be given that will be satisfactory. The old opinion, that a blow must require blood, is not of force. Blows may be compromised in many cases. What those cases are, must depend on the seconds.

APPENDIX.

Since the foregoing Code was in the press, a friend has favored me with the *IRISH CODE OF HONOR*, which I had never seen, and it is published as an appendix to it.—One thing must be apparent to every reader, viz, the marked amelioration of the rules that govern in duelling at the present time. I am unable to say what code exists now in Ireland, but I very much doubt whether it be of the same character which it bore in 1777. The "American Quarterly Review," for September, 1824, in a notice of Sir Jonah Barrington's history of his own times, has published this code, and followed it up with some remarks, which I have thought proper to insert also.[1] The grave reviewer has spoken of certain States in terms so unlike a gentleman, that I would advise him to look at home, and say whether he does not think that the manners of his own countrymen do not require great amendment. I am very sure that the citizens of the States so disrespectfully spoken of, would feel a deep humiliation to be compelled to exchange their urbanity of deportment for the uncouth incivility of the people of Massachusetts. Look at their public journals, and you will find them, very generally, teeming with abuse of private character, which would not be countenanced here. The idea of New England becoming a school for manners is about as fanciful as Bolingbroke's "idea of a patriot king." I like their *fortiter in re*, but utterly eschew their *suaviter in modo*:

The practice of Duelling, and points of honor, settled at Clonmell summer assizes, 1777, by the gentlemen delegates of Tipperary, Galway, Mayo, Sligo and Roscommon, and prescribed for general adoption throughout Ireland:

RULE 1. The first offence requires the first apology, al-

[1] These remarks were not included in the 1838 edition of Wilson's code.—JKW

though the retort may have been more offensive than the insult; example: A tells B he is impertinent, &c., and B. retorts that he lies; yet A must make the first apology, because he gave the first offence, and then (after one fire) B may explain away the retort by subsequent apology.

RULE 2. But if the parties would rather fight on, then, after two shots each, (but in no case before,) B may explain first, and A apologize afterwards.

N.B. The above rules apply to all cases of offences in retort, not of a stronger class than the example.

RULE 3. If a doubt exist who gave the first offence, the decision rests with the seconds. If they *won't* decide, or *can't* agree, the matter must proceed to two shots, or a hit, if the challenger requires it.

RULE 4. When the *lie direct* is the first offence, the aggressor must either beg pardon in express terms, exchange two shots previous to apology, or three shots followed up by explanation, or fire on till a severe hit be received by one party or the other.

RULE 5. As a blow is strictly prohibited under any circumstances among gentlemen, no verbal apology can be received for such an insult. The alternatives, therefore, are: the offender handing a cane to the injured party, to be used on his own back, at the same time begging pardon; firing on until one or both is disabled; or exchanging three shots, and then asking pardon *without* the proffer of the *cane*.

If swords are used, the parties engage till one is well blooded, disabled or disarmed; or until, after receiving a wound, and blood being drawn, the aggressor begs pardon.

N.B. A disarm is considered the same as a disable; the disarmer may (strictly) break his adversary's sword; but if it be the challenger who is disarmed, it is considered ungenerous to do so.

In case the challenged be disarmed and refuses to ask pardon or atone, he must not be *killed*, as formerly; but the challenger may lay his own sword on the aggressor's shoulder, then break the aggressor's sword, and say, "I spare your life!" The challenged can never revive the quarrel, the challenger may.

RULE 6. If A gives B the lie, and B retorts by a blow, (being the two greatest offences) no reconciliation *can* take place till after two discharges each, or a severe hit; after which,

B may beg A's pardon for the blow, and then A may explain simply for the lie; because a blow is *never* allowable, and the offence of the lie therefore merges in it. (See preceding rule.)

N.B. Challenges for undivulged causes may be reconciled on the ground, after one shot. An explanation, or the slightest hit, should be sufficient in such cases, because no personal offence transpired.

RULE 7. But no apology can be received, in any case, after the parties have actually taken their ground, without exchange of fires.

RULE 8. In the above case, no challenger is obliged to divulge the cause of his challenge (if private) unless required by the challenged to do so *before* their meeting.

RULE 9. All imputations of cheating at play, races, &c., to be considered equivalent to a blow; but may be reconciled after one shot, on admitting their falsehood, and begging pardon publicly.

RULE 10. Any insult to a lady under a gentleman's care or protection, to be considered as, by one degree, a greater offence than if given to the gentleman personally, and to be regulated accordingly.

RULE 11. Offences originating or accruing from the support of ladies' reputation, to be considered as less unjustifiable than any others of the same class, and as admitting of slighter apologies by the aggressor. This to be determined by the circumstances of the case, but *always* favorably to the lady.

RULE 12. In simple unpremeditated recontres with the small sword or couteau-de-chasse, the rule is, first draw, first sheath, unless blood be drawn; then both sheath, and proceed to investigation.

RULE 13. No dumb-shooting, or firing in the air, admissible in any case. The challenger ought not to have challenged without receiving offence; and the challenged ought, if he gave offence, to have made an apology before he came on the ground; therefore children's play must be dishonorable on one side or the other, and is accordingly prohibited.

RULE 14. Seconds to be of equal rank in society with the principals they attend, inasmuch as a second may choose or chance to become a principal, and equality is indispensable.

RULE 15. Challenges are never to be delivered at night, unless the party to be challenged intend leaving the place of offence before morning; for it is desirable to avoid all hot-headed proceedings.

RULE 16. The challenged has the right to choose his own weapon, unless the challenger gives his honor he is no swordsman; after which, however, he cannot decline any second species of weapon proposed by the challenged.

RULE 17. The challenged chooses his ground; the challenger chooses his distance; the seconds fix the time and terms of firing.

RULE 18. The seconds load in presence of each other, unless they give their mutual honors that they have charged smooth and single, which should be held sufficient.

RULE 19. Firing may be regulated, first by signal; secondly, by word of command; or thirdly at pleasure, as may be agreeable to the parties. In the latter case the parties may fire at their reasonable leisure, but second presents and rests are strictly prohibited.

RULE 20. In all cases a miss-fire is equivalent to a shot, and a snap or a non-cock is to be considered as a miss-fire.

RULE 21. Seconds are bound to attempt a reconciliation before the meeting takes place, or after sufficient firing or hits, as specified.

RULE 22. Any wound sufficient to agitate the nerves and necessarily make the hands shake, must end the business for that day.

RULE 23. If the cause of meeting be of such a nature that no apology or explanation can or will be received, the challenged takes his ground, and calls on the challenger to proceed as he chooses; in such cases, firing at pleasure is the usual practice, but may be varied by agreement.

RULE 24. In slight cases, the second hands his principal but one pistol, but in gross cases, two, holding another case ready-charged in reserve.

RULE 25. When seconds disagree, and resolve to exchange shots themselves, it must be at the same time, and at right angles with their principals.

If with swords, side by side, at five paces interval.

N.B. All matters and doubts not herein mentioned, will be explained and cleared up by application to the committee, who meet alternately at Clonmell and Galway, at the quarter sessions, for the purpose.

CROW RYAN, President.

James Keogh, } Secretaries
Amby Bodkin, }

ADDITIONAL GALWAY ARTICLES.

"RULE 1. No party can be allowed to bend his knee or cover his side with his left hand; but may present at any level from the hip to the eye.

"RULE 2. One can either advance or retreat, if the ground be measured. If the ground be measured, either party may advance at pleasure, even to touch muzzle—but neither can advance on his adversary after the fire, unless his adversary step forward on him.

"The seconds stand responsible for this last rule being strictly observed; bad cases have accrued from neglecting it."

This precise and enlightened digest was rendered necessary by the multitude of quarrels that arose without "sufficiently *dignified* provocation." The *point of honor* men required a uniform government; and the code thus formed was disseminated throughout the island, with directions that it should be strictly observed by all gentlemen, and kept in their pistol-cases. The rules, with some others, were commonly styled "the thirty-six commandments," and according to our author, have been much acted upon down to the present day. Tipperary and Galway were the chief schools of duelling. We remember to have heard, in travelling to the town of the former name in a stage-coach, a dispute between two Irish companions, on the point, which was the most "gentlemanly" county in all Ireland —Tipperary or Galway?—and both laid great stress upon the relative duelling merits of those counties.

Bibliographic Notes

DUELING has been a topic of interest to many writers, and the literature about the duel in America is substantial and varied. Much of the printed material, unfortunately, is of limited value, consisting of tracts, sermons, or booklets designed either to condemn duelists or to defend them. General historical accounts of dueling extending beyond the American experience date from at least 1841, when John C. Milligen's *The History of Duelling* was published in London in two volumes. Another such study, dated 1868, is Andrew Stienmetz, *The Romance of Duelling in All Times and Countries* (London, 2 vols.).

Perhaps the first noteworthy American book on the duel was Lorenzo Sabine, *Notes on Duels and Duelling* (Boston: Crosby, Nichols & Co., 1855). Still available in most libraries, Sabine's rambling account has considerable merit. It has been superceded, however, as a reference by two twentieth-century books: Harnett T. Kane, *Gentlemen, Swords and Pistols* (New York: William Morris & Co., 1951), and Don. C. Seitz, *Famous American Duels* (Freeport, N.Y., 1966).

The Seitz volume was first published in 1929 by Thomas Y. Crowell and has been reprinted by Books for Libraries Press. The book well deserves that attention. The author devoted two excellent chapters to the history and development of dueling in America, then discussed in depth fourteen duels ranging in significance from the Aaron Burr–Alexander Hamilton disaster to the lesser-known David Terry–David Broderick fracas. Seitz, who died in 1935, was a skillful writer, author of more than thirty volumes in history. His readable book on dueling is a standard bibliographic entry in the social history of the United States.

Harnett Kane's twenty entertaining chapters deal lightly and at times humorously with duels and duelists. He has written numerous books of popular history, many of them about his delightful Louisiana delta country. His dueling stories are spicey, citable, and worthwhile to the serious student of the code, if not as historically precise as one might like. Kane includes a good bibliography. His literary style is racy and sparkling—different in many ways from that of Seitz, who is much more straightforward with his prose.

Two additional books containing general information on the American duel are Lewis S. Benjamin, *Famous Duels and Assassinations* (New York: J. H. Sears, 1930), and William O. Stevens, *Pistols at Ten Paces: The Story of the Code of Honor in America* (Boston: Houghton Mifflin Co., 1940). The Benjamin book is mediocre, while the Stevens volume is very good.

Several books and journal articles have been written about the duel in specific states and cities of the South. A number of these items were useful in my research. Robert R. Howison has a fine article, "Duelling in Virginia," in *William and Mary Quarterly Historical Magazine*, 2d ser. 4 (October, 1924) : 217–244, and Archibald W. Patterson is author of the informative *The Code Duello, With Special Reference to Virginia* (Richmond: Richmond Press, Inc., 1927). I have an article, "The Code of Honor in Ante-Bellum South Carolina," in *South Carolina Historical Magazine* 54 (July, 1953) : 113–128. An old but nonetheless useful item on North Carolina is S. B. Weeks, "The Code in North Carolina," *Magazine of American History* 26 (February, 1891) : 443. An outstanding item about a single duel fought in North-Carolina style—and highly illustrative of dueling in the upper South—is Henry W. Lewis, "The Dugger-Dromgoole Duel," *North Carolina Historical Review* 34 (July, 1934) : 327–345.

Stuart Landry's *Duelling in Old New Orleans* (New Orleans: Pelican Publishing Co., 1950) is perhaps the best of several accounts of duels in that warm nest of sword and pistol experts. John S. Kendall's "According to the Code," *Louisiana Historical Quarterly* 23 (January, 1940) : 141–161, is a carefully researched, nicely written item. Two aged but informative journal articles on dueling in the New Orleans area are John Augustin, "The Old Duelling Grounds of New Orleans," *Arts and Letters* 1 (August, 1887), and Louis Meader, "Duelling in the Old Creole Days," *Century* 74 (June, 1907) : 248–259.

Dueling in Maryland and the District of Columbia has been the subject of three outdated but worthy articles. Milton T. Adkins wrote "The Bladensburg Duelling Ground," *Magazine of American History* 25 (January, 1891) : 18. William J. Maddox's "Bladensburg, the Old Duelling Ground," *Catholic*

World 126 (November, 1927): 234–239, is a more complete study. Myra L. Spaulding was author of the interesting "Duelling in the District of Columbia," *Records of the Columbia Historical Society*, 1928. The story of the duel in the federal district is largely the story of Southern congressmen giving or accepting challenges, of course.

By far the best work dealing with the duel in a single city or state is Thomas Gamble, *Savannah Duels and Duellists, 1733–1877* (Savannah: Review Publishing and Printing Co., 1923). Gamble's book was an obvious labor of love by the author—love for the South and especially the state of Georgia. His quotes are without documentation but are clearly the results of serious research, especially in newspaper files. His book is carefully written, accurate, and delightfully old-fashioned and ministerial in style. His book is the source for many of the dueling incidents I have reported.

As my footnotes indicate, I made much use of travelers' journals, written by English citizens and others who came to America during the antebellum years. These visitors arrived in increasing numbers after the Treaty of Ghent had been signed in 1815, and they were impressed and often amused by the American life-style. Dueling caught their attention, of course, and they wrote about duels in their diaries and journals. While the travelers' accounts are excellent sources for social history, they must be used with caution, since short-term visitors were given to exaggeration and repetition of hearsay. Travelers whose published accounts contain reports of dueling incidents include the following: John Pope, *A Tour through the Southern and Western Territories of the United States of North America* (New York: Arno, 1971; originally published in 1792); J. Cooper, *Notions of the Americans*, 2 vols. (London: Colburn & Co., 1828); Harriet Martineau, *Society in America*, 3 vols. (London: Saunders & Otley, 1837); William Faux, *Memorable Days in America* (London: Simpkin & Marshall, 1823); James Silk Buckingham, *The Slave States of America*, 2 vols. (London: Fisher, Son & Co., 1842); Frances A. Kemble, *Journal of a Residence on a Georgia Plantation in 1838 and 1839* (New York: Harper & Bros., 1863); Charles Lyell, *A Second Visit to the United States of North America*, 2 vols. (New York: Harper & Bros., 1849); James Stirling, *Letters from the Slave States* (London: Richard Bentley, 1857); Tyrone Power, *Impressions of America*, 2 vols. (London: Richard Bentley, 1836); F. D. Scott, ed., *Baron Klinkowström's America, 1818-1820*

(Evanston: Northwestern University Press, 1952); Charles W. Janson, *The Stranger in America, 1793–1806* (New York: Burt Franklin, 1971; originally published in 1807); Alex[ander] Mackay, *The Western World; or, Travels in the United States in 1846–47*, 2 vols. (London: Richard Bentley, 1849); George W. Featherstonhaugh, *Excursion through the Slave States from Washington on the Potomac to the Frontier of Mexico*, 2 vols. (London: John Murray, 1844); Benjamin Latrobe, *The Journal of Benjamin Latrobe* (New York: D. Appleton, 1905); and Frederick Marryat, *A Diary in America with Remarks on Its Institutions*, ed. Sydney Jackman (New York: Alfred A. Knopf, 1962).

From the list, Harriet Martineau, famed literary personage, has especially pungent comments about Americans. Tyrone Power, the popular actor, gives easy reading—interesting and accurate. James Silk Buckingham wrote with much attention to detail and reported skillfully on interviews with Americans of the less-favored classes. James Stirling recounts in hypercritical language various episodes, some of them obviously hearsay. Alexander Mackay, like Buckingham, gives a fine report of what he has heard and is dependable, and Frederick Marryat has separate chapters devoted to particular social customs, making his diary unusually valuable. Frances Kemble (Mrs. Pierce Butler) probably should be classified a resident rather than a visitor. Her volume is a prejudiced account of Southern plantation life, written after she had divorced her husband, a wealthy Georgia planter.

Another American who wrote well about a two-year stay in the South was Bishop Henry Whipple. His diary, *Bishop Whipple's Southern Diary, 1843–44*, edited by Lester Shippee, (New York: D. A. Capo Press, 1968), is lucid and critical regarding Southern customs and attitudes.

There was humor in the dueling story, although it was much outweighed by the pathos and tragedy. Two volumes that offer humorous approaches to the duel and other institutions are Fairfax Downey, *Our Lusty Forefathers* (New York: Charles Scribner's Sons, 1947), and Arthur P. Hudson, *Humor of the Old Deep South* (New York: Macmillan Co., 1936). Both books are well written, but Hudson's volume is the better of the two.

Dueling attracted numerous pamphlet and tract writers. Their pithy offerings are of value as indicators of pro- and anti-duel sentiment—and of the state of the art of pamphleteering. A representative sampling includes Mason Locke Weems, *God's Revenge Against Duelling* (Philadelphia: privately printed, 1827); Giacomo Sega, *An Essay on the Practice of Duelling* (Philadelphia: privately printed, 1830); John L. Wilson, *The Code of Honor; or, Rules for the Government of Principals and Seconds in Duelling* (Charleston: James Phinney, 1838); William Jay, *An Essay on Duelling* (Savannah: Savannah Anti-duelling Association, 1829); E. B. C. Cash, *The Cash-Shannon Duel* (Greenville, S.C.: privately printed, 1881); Arthur Wigfall, *Sermon Upon Duelling. Together With the Constitution of the Grahamville Association for the Suppression of Duelling* (Charleston: privately printed, 1856); Nathaniel D. Bowen, *A Sermon; Preached October, 1807, in St. Michael's Church, Charleston* (Charleston: privately printed, 1823); and William H. Barnwell, *The Impiety and Absurdity of Duelling—a Sermon* (Charleston: Walker & Burke, 1844). A number of pamphlets such as these are with the Yates Snowden papers at the South Caroliniana Library, Columbia, South Carolina.

In my writing I made much use of John Hope Franklin's superb study, *The Militant South* (Cambridge: Harvard University Press, 1956). Franklin is one of the nation's premier historians, *From Slavery to Freedom* (New York: A. A. Knopf, 1947) being perhaps his best-known work. *The Militant South* has tremendous chapters on the Southerner's proneness to violence and his love for military trappings—and one rich chapter on dueling and other forms of personal combat in vogue before the Civil War.

Finally, I have a heavy debt (as does anyone who studies the American South) to the scholarship of Clement Eaton, one of the most prominent American regional historians. In three of his half-dozen major volumes, *The Freedom of Thought Struggle in the Old South* (New York: Harper & Row, 1964; originally published in 1940), *A History of the Old South* (3rd ed. published in New York by Macmillan Co. in 1975; first published in 1949), and *The Growth of Southern Civilization* (New York: Harper Torchbooks, 1961), he presents provocative observations about the complexity of Southern society and social devices. In his own words, Clement Eaton is "concerned with people rather than vague and impersonal forces." His histories, as a result, are at once sensitive and enriching. Eaton, like Bell Irwin Wiley, remarkable teacher and historian of the American Civil War, knows how to make history come alive.

CPSIA information can be obtained at www.ICGtesting.com
Printed in the USA
BVOW05s1350020414

349519BV00002B/426/P